Mediterranean Instant Pot Cookbook for Beginners:

150 Easy-to-Make Mediterranean Diet Recipes for Healthy and Quick Meals Every Day

Table of Contents

Basic Broths & Stocks ... 7
- Quick Vegetable Broth ... 7
- Express Chicken Bone Broth ... 7
- Instant Seafood Stock ... 8
- Rosemary-Infused Beef Broth ... 8
- Herbed Tomato Base Stock ... 9
- Pressure-Cooked Mushroom Broth ... 9
- Garlic & Herb Infusion ... 10
- Lamb Bone Broth Elixir ... 10
- Onion & Celery Base ... 11
- Mediterranean Spice Broth ... 11

Wholesome Whole Grains ... 12
- Quinoa & Olive Salad ... 12
- Instant Farro & Vegetable Medley ... 12
- Couscous with Caramelized Onions ... 13
- Bulgur Wheat Pilaf with Herbs ... 13
- Instant Pot Orzo with Lemon ... 14
- Saffron Millet Delight ... 14
- Barley & Vegetable Risotto ... 15
- Express Mediterranean Rice ... 15
- Moroccan Spiced Freekeh ... 16
- Herb-Infused Sorghum ... 16

Vegetable Delights ... 17
- Stuffed Eggplants with Rice ... 17
- Mediterranean Vegetable Curry ... 17
- Instant Ratatouille ... 18
- Zucchini & Tomato Medley ... 18
- Artichoke & Lemon Stew ... 19
- Roasted Red Pepper Soup ... 19
- Spinach & Feta Stuffed Tomatoes ... 20
- Pressure-Cooked Mediterranean Veggie Mix ... 20
- Olive & Capers Veggie Toss ... 21
- Potato & Green Beans in Tomato Sauce ... 21

Seafood Sensations ... 22
- Quick Seafood Paella ... 22
- Instant Pot Shrimp Scampi ... 22
- Lemon Herb Fish Fillets ... 23
- Pressure-Cooked Mussels in White Wine ... 23
- Mediterranean Octopus Salad ... 24

- Clams in Spicy Tomato Sauce ... 24
- Olive Oil & Garlic Braised Calamari ... 25
- Instant Tuna & Caper Stew ... 25
- Fish Tagine with Olives ... 26
- Quick Seafood Risotto ... 26

Poultry & Meats ... 27
- Chicken Tagine with Preserved Lemons ... 27
- Lamb Shanks in Tomato Sauce ... 27
- Pressure-Cooked Beef Gyros ... 28
- Instant Pot Herb-Roasted Chicken ... 28
- Mediterranean Pork Ribs ... 29
- Chicken Kofta with Yogurt Sauce ... 29
- Beef & Olive Stew ... 30
- Quick Chicken Souvlaki ... 30
- Braised Duck with Oranges & Olives ... 31
- Lamb & Chickpea Curry ... 31

Legumes & Lentils ... 32
- Instant Pot Lentil Soup ... 32
- Chickpea & Spinach Masala ... 32
- Mediterranean Bean Stew ... 33
- Lentils with Chorizo & Vegetables ... 33
- Quick Falafel Mix ... 34
- White Bean & Herb Soup ... 34
- Black Eyed Peas in Tomato Sauce ... 35
- Instant Pot Hummus ... 35
- Chickpea & Saffron Soup ... 36
- Lentil & Vegetable Medley ... 36

Pasta & Risottos ... 37
- Instant Seafood Linguine ... 37
- Mushroom & Truffle Risotto ... 37
- Pasta Puttanesca in a Flash ... 38
- Pressure-Cooked Orzo & Shrimp ... 38
- Tomato & Basil Penne ... 39
- Creamy Spinach Risotto ... 39
- Mediterranean Mac 'n' Cheese ... 40
- Spaghetti with Instant Meatballs ... 40
- Sausage & Pepper Pasta ... 41
- Lemon & Asparagus Risotto ... 41

Soups & Stews ... 42
- Minestrone in Minutes ... 42

- Instant Pot Bouillabaisse ... 42
- The Quick Version ... 43
  - Eggplant & Lentil Soup ... 43
  - Chilled Cucumber & Yogurt Soup ... 43
  - Instant Pot Fisherman's Stew ... 44
  - Chickpea & Spinach Soup ... 44
  - Lamb & Vegetable Stew ... 45
  - Mediterranean Broth with Pasta & Beans ... 45
  - Spicy Tomato & Chorizo Soup ... 46
- Sauces & Dips ... 47
  - Quick Tzatziki ... 47
  - Instant Pot Romesco Sauce ... 47
  - Garlic & Herb Olive Spread ... 48
  - Pressure-Cooked Marinara ... 48
  - Tapenade in a Flash ... 49
  - Instant Muhammara ... 49
  - Mediterranean Pesto Sauce ... 50
  - Whipped Feta with Roasted Peppers ... 50
  - Quick & Creamy Hummus ... 51
  - Spiced Tomato & Almond Dip ... 51
- Classic Mediterranean Salads ... 52
  - Pressure-Cooked Potato Salad ... 52
  - Quick Couscous & Vegetable Salad ... 52
  - Instant Pot Tabouleh ... 53
  - Chickpea & Roasted Pepper Salad ... 53
  - Mediterranean Beet Salad ... 54
  - Fennel & Citrus Medley ... 54
  - Warm Lentil & Herb Salad ... 55
  - Tomato, Mozzarella & Basil Salad ... 55
  - Orzo & Spinach Salad ... 56
  - Pressure-Cooked Artichoke Salad ... 56
- Delightful Desserts ... 57
  - Instant Pot Flan ... 57
  - Pressure-Cooked Rice Pudding ... 57
  - Mediterranean Cheesecake ... 58
  - Quick Poached Pears in Wine ... 58
  - Olive Oil & Lemon Cake ... 59
  - Almond & Fig Tart ... 59
  - Instant Pot Baklava Pudding ... 60
  - Creamy Orange & Chocolate Pots ... 60

- Pistachio & Honey Crème Brûlée 61
- Quick Berry & Mascarpone Delight 61

Dairy & Cheese Magic 62
- Instant Pot Feta & Spinach Dip 62
- Creamy Ricotta in Minutes 62
- Mediterranean Queso Fundido 63
- Quick Mozzarella & Tomato Melt 63
- Labneh with Olive Oil & Za'atar 64
- Pressure-Cooked Cheese Fondue 64
- Herb & Garlic Cream Cheese Spread 65
- Instant Pot Paneer 65
- Mediterranean Yogurt with Nuts & Honey 66
- Brie & Roasted Garlic Dip 66

Flavorful Sides & Accents 67
- Olive & Herb Focaccia 67
- Garlic & Parmesan Mashed Potatoes 67
- Instant Marinated Olives 68
- Mediterranean Pickled Vegetables 68
- Pressure-Cooked Polenta with Sun-Dried Tomatoes 69
- Lemon & Herb Roasted Carrots 69
- Quick Mediterranean Slaw 70
- Tomato & Basil Bruschetta 70
- Herbed Butter Beans 71
- Instant Pot Stuffed Grape Leaves 71

Holiday & Festive Feasts 72
- Instant Pot Lamb for Easter 72
- Quick Mediterranean Stuffed Turkey 72
- Pressure-Cooked Christmas Seafood Medley 73
- Festive Olive & Fig Roast Pork 73
- Holiday Beef & Olive Tagine 74
- Instant New Year's Lentil Stew 74
- Chicken with Dates & Pistachios 75
- Mediterranean Festive Vegetable Platter 75
- Lamb & Apricot for Eid Celebrations 76
- Quick Festive Mediterranean Rice 76

Quick Mediterranean Bites 77
- Instant Pot Greek Meatballs 77
- Pressure-Cooked Stuffed Mushrooms 77
- Quick Olive & Cheese Pinwheels 78
- Instant Pot Falafel 78

Mediterranean Tapas Platter ... 79
Quick Spinach & Cheese Triangles ... 79
Pressure-Cooked Garlic Shrimp ... 80
Mediterranean Quesadillas ... 80
Olive & Tomato Mini Pizzas ... 81
Instant Pot Mini Lamb Pies ... 81

Basic Broths & Stocks

Quick Vegetable Broth

Yield: 4 servings | Prep time: 15 minutes | Cook time: 25 minutes

Ingredients:

- 1 large onion, quartered (skin on for deeper color)
- 2 carrots, chopped into large pieces
- 2 celery stalks, chopped
- 4 garlic cloves, smashed
- 1 bay leaf
- 1 tsp dried thyme
- 2 tsp salt (adjust to taste)
- 1/2 tsp black peppercorns
- 1 small bunch parsley
- 6 cups water

Directions:

1. Add all the ingredients into the Instant Pot.
2. Secure the lid and set the Instant Pot to the "Manual" or "Pressure Cook" setting. Cook for 15 minutes at high pressure.
3. Once done, let the pressure release naturally for 10 minutes, then quick release any remaining pressure.
4. Strain the broth into a large bowl or container, discarding the vegetables.
5. Adjust seasoning if necessary and use as desired or store in the refrigerator for up to 5 days.

Nutritional Information: 40 calories, 1g protein, 10g carbohydrates, 0.1g fat, 2g fiber, 0mg cholesterol, 590mg sodium, 220mg potassium.

Express Chicken Bone Broth

Yield: 4 servings | Prep time: 10 minutes | Cook time: 45 minutes

Ingredients:

- 2 lbs chicken bones (a mix of necks, backs, and feet provides the best gelatin content)
- 1 onion, quartered
- 2 celery stalks, chopped
- 1 carrot, chopped
- 4 garlic cloves, smashed
- 1 bay leaf
- 1 tsp dried rosemary
- 1 tsp salt (adjust to taste)
- 1/2 tsp black peppercorns
- 1 small bunch parsley
- 1 tablespoon apple cider vinegar (helps to extract minerals from bones)
- 8 cups water

Directions:

1. Place all ingredients into the Instant Pot.
2. Secure the lid and set the Instant Pot to the "Manual" or "Pressure Cook" setting. Cook for 45 minutes at high pressure.
3. Once done, let the pressure release naturally.
4. Strain the broth into a large bowl or container, discarding the bones and vegetables.
5. Adjust seasoning if necessary and use immediately, or let cool and store in the refrigerator for up to 5 days.

Nutritional Information: 35 calories, 6g protein, 2g carbohydrates, 0.5g fat, 0.5g fiber, 15mg cholesterol, 650mg sodium, 120mg potassium.

Instant Seafood Stock

Yield: 4 servings | Prep time: 10 minutes | Cook time: 20 minutes

Ingredients:

- 1 lb seafood scraps (shrimp shells, fish bones, crab shells, etc.)
- 1 onion, quartered
- 2 celery stalks, chopped
- 1 carrot, chopped
- 4 garlic cloves, smashed
- 1 bay leaf
- 1/2 tsp dried thyme
- 1 tsp salt (adjust to taste)
- 1/2 tsp black peppercorns
- 1 small bunch parsley
- 1 tablespoon tomato paste
- 7 cups water
- 1/2 cup dry white wine (like Pinot Grigio)

Directions:

1. Combine all ingredients in the Instant Pot.
2. Seal the lid and set the Instant Pot to the "Manual" or "Pressure Cook" setting. Cook for 20 minutes at high pressure.
3. Once completed, allow for a natural pressure release.
4. Strain the stock through a fine-mesh sieve, discarding the solids.
5. Adjust seasoning if desired and use as needed or store in the refrigerator for up to 3 days.

Nutritional Information: 45 calories, 5g protein, 4g carbohydrates, 0.2g fat, 1g fiber, 20mg cholesterol, 680mg sodium, 180mg potassium.

Rosemary-Infused Beef Broth

Yield: 4 servings | Prep time: 15 minutes | Cook time: 60 minutes

Ingredients:

- 2 lbs beef bones (like marrow, knuckles, and rib bones)
- 1 onion, quartered
- 2 celery stalks, chopped
- 1 carrot, chopped
- 4 garlic cloves, smashed
- 2 bay leaves
- 2 sprigs fresh rosemary
- 1 tsp salt (adjust to taste)
- 1/2 tsp black peppercorns
- 1 tablespoon apple cider vinegar (helps to extract minerals from bones)
- 8 cups water

Directions:

1. First, blanch the beef bones: place them in the Instant Pot, cover with water, and set to "Sauté" for 10 minutes. Drain and rinse.
2. Add the blanched bones back into the pot along with the other ingredients.
3. Secure the lid and set the Instant Pot to the "Manual" or "Pressure Cook" setting. Cook for 60 minutes at high pressure.
4. After the cycle is complete, allow for a natural pressure release.
5. Strain the broth, discarding solids. Adjust seasoning if needed, and use immediately or store in the refrigerator for up to 5 days.

Nutritional Information: 50 calories, 7g protein, 3g carbohydrates, 1g fat, 1g fiber, 20mg cholesterol, 700mg sodium, 200mg potassium.

Herbed Tomato Base Stock

Yield: 4 servings | Prep time: 10 minutes | Cook time: 25 minutes

Ingredients:

- 5 large ripe tomatoes, quartered
- 1 onion, quartered
- 2 celery stalks, chopped
- 1 carrot, chopped
- 4 garlic cloves, smashed
- 2 bay leaves
- 2 sprigs fresh basil
- 2 sprigs fresh oregano
- 1 tsp salt (adjust to taste)
- 1/2 tsp black peppercorns
- 6 cups water

Directions:

1. Combine tomatoes, onion, celery, carrot, garlic, herbs, salt, peppercorns, and water in the Instant Pot.
2. Secure the lid and set the Instant Pot to the "Manual" or "Pressure Cook" setting. Cook for 25 minutes at high pressure.
3. Once done, let the pressure release naturally for about 10 minutes, then quick release any remaining pressure.
4. Strain the stock through a fine-mesh sieve, discarding the solids. Adjust seasoning if necessary and use as a base for soups, stews, or sauces, or store in the refrigerator for up to 5 days.

Nutritional Information: 40 calories, 1.5g protein, 9g carbohydrates, 0.3g fat, 2.5g fiber, 0mg cholesterol, 620mg sodium, 400mg potassium.

Pressure-Cooked Mushroom Broth

Yield: 4 servings | Prep time: 15 minutes | Cook time: 30 minutes

Ingredients:

- 1 lb mixed fresh mushrooms (like shiitake, cremini, and portobello), coarsely chopped
- 1 onion, quartered
- 2 celery stalks, chopped
- 1 carrot, chopped
- 4 garlic cloves, smashed
- 2 bay leaves
- 1 sprig fresh thyme
- 1 tsp salt (adjust to taste)
- 1/2 tsp black peppercorns
- 6 cups water

Directions:

1. Add mushrooms, onion, celery, carrot, garlic, bay leaves, thyme, salt, peppercorns, and water into the Instant Pot.
2. Seal the lid and set the Instant Pot to the "Manual" or "Pressure Cook" setting. Cook for 30 minutes at high pressure.
3. Once done, allow for a natural pressure release for about 10 minutes, then quick release any remaining pressure.
4. Strain the broth through a fine-mesh sieve, discarding the solids. Adjust seasoning if necessary and use immediately or store in the refrigerator for up to 5 days.

Nutritional Information: 25 calories, 2g protein, 5g carbohydrates, 0.2g fat, 1.5g fiber, 0mg cholesterol, 610mg sodium, 250mg potassium.

Garlic & Herb Infusion

Yield: 4 servings | Prep time: 5 minutes | Cook time: 20 minutes

Ingredients:

- 8 garlic cloves, smashed
- 1 sprig fresh rosemary
- 1 sprig fresh thyme
- 1 sprig fresh basil
- 1 sprig fresh oregano
- 4 cups water
- 1/2 tsp salt (adjust to taste)
- 1/2 tsp black peppercorns

Directions:

1. Combine garlic, rosemary, thyme, basil, oregano, salt, peppercorns, and water in the Instant Pot.
2. Secure the lid and set the Instant Pot to the "Manual" or "Pressure Cook" setting. Cook for 20 minutes at high pressure.
3. Once done, allow for a natural pressure release for about 10 minutes, then quick release any remaining pressure.
4. Strain the infusion through a fine-mesh sieve, discarding the solids. Adjust seasoning if necessary and enjoy as a flavorful drink, use as a base for soups or sauces, or store in the refrigerator for up to 3 days.

Nutritional Information: 5 calories, 0.2g protein, 1g carbohydrates, 0g fat, 0.2g fiber, 0mg cholesterol, 300mg sodium, 20mg potassium.

Lamb Bone Broth Elixir

Yield: 4 servings | Prep time: 10 minutes | Cook time: 120 minutes

Ingredients:

- 2 lbs lamb bones
- 1 onion, quartered
- 2 celery stalks, chopped
- 2 carrots, chopped
- 4 garlic cloves, smashed
- 1 bay leaf
- 2 sprigs fresh rosemary
- 1 tsp black peppercorns
- 1 tbsp apple cider vinegar (helps extract minerals from the bones)
- 6 cups water
- Salt to taste

Directions:

1. Place lamb bones, onion, celery, carrot, garlic, bay leaf, rosemary, peppercorns, and apple cider vinegar into the Instant Pot.
2. Pour in the water, ensuring that the bones are submerged but not exceeding the maximum fill line of the pot.
3. Secure the lid and set the Instant Pot to the "Manual" or "Pressure Cook" setting. Cook for 120 minutes at high pressure.
4. Once done, allow for a natural pressure release. Strain the broth through a fine-mesh sieve, discarding the solids. Season with salt as desired. Store in the refrigerator for up to 5 days or freeze for longer storage.

Nutritional Information: 50 calories, 7g protein, 2g carbohydrates, 1.5g fat, 0.5g fiber, 15mg cholesterol, 85mg sodium, 120mg potassium.

Onion & Celery Base

Yield: 4 servings | Prep time: 10 minutes | Cook time: 25 minutes

Ingredients:

- 4 large onions, coarsely chopped
- 4 celery stalks, coarsely chopped
- 2 tbsp olive oil
- 1 tsp salt (adjust to taste)
- 1/2 tsp black pepper
- 5 cups water

Directions:

1. Turn the Instant Pot to the "Sauté" function and add the olive oil. Once hot, add in the onions and celery. Cook, stirring occasionally, until the onions become translucent, about 5-7 minutes.
2. Season with salt and pepper, then pour in the water, ensuring the vegetables are submerged.
3. Secure the lid and set the Instant Pot to the "Manual" or "Pressure Cook" setting. Cook for 18 minutes at high pressure.
4. Once done, allow for a quick pressure release. Strain the base through a fine-mesh sieve, discarding the solids. Use immediately or store in the refrigerator for up to 5 days.

Nutritional Information: 80 calories, 1.5g protein, 12g carbohydrates, 3.5g fat, 2.5g fiber, 0mg cholesterol, 620mg sodium, 220mg potassium.

Mediterranean Spice Broth

Yield: 4 servings | Prep time: 15 minutes | Cook time: 30 minutes

Ingredients:

- 6 cups water
- 2 cinnamon sticks
- 4 cloves
- 1 tsp coriander seeds
- 1 tsp cumin seeds
- 1/2 tsp fennel seeds
- 1 bay leaf
- 1 star anise
- 2 cardamom pods, crushed
- 1 inch piece of fresh ginger, sliced
- 2 garlic cloves, smashed
- Salt to taste

Directions:

1. Place all ingredients into the Instant Pot.
2. Secure the lid and set the Instant Pot to the "Manual" or "Pressure Cook" setting. Cook for 30 minutes at high pressure.
3. Once done, allow for a natural pressure release. Strain the broth through a fine-mesh sieve, discarding the spices. Season with salt as desired. Store in the refrigerator for up to 5 days or freeze for longer storage.

Nutritional Information: 10 calories, 0.2g protein, 2g carbohydrates, 0.1g fat, 0.5g fiber, 0mg cholesterol, 10mg sodium, 30mg potassium.

Wholesome Whole Grains

Quinoa & Olive Salad

Yield: 4 servings | Prep time: 10 minutes | Cook time: 12 minutes

Ingredients:

- 1 cup quinoa, rinsed and drained
- 1 1/4 cups water
- 1/2 cup Kalamata olives, pitted and halved
- 1/2 cup cherry tomatoes, halved
- 1/4 cup red onion, finely chopped
- 1/4 cup feta cheese, crumbled
- 1/4 cup fresh parsley, chopped
- 3 tbsp olive oil
- 2 tbsp lemon juice
- 1 clove garlic, minced
- Salt and pepper to taste

Directions:

1. In the Instant Pot, combine quinoa and water. Secure the lid and set the pot to the "Manual" or "Pressure Cook" setting. Cook for 1 minute at high pressure. Allow a natural release for 10 minutes, then perform a quick release. Fluff the quinoa with a fork.
2. Transfer the cooked quinoa to a large mixing bowl and allow it to cool slightly.
3. Add olives, cherry tomatoes, red onion, feta cheese, and parsley to the bowl. In a separate small bowl, whisk together olive oil, lemon juice, minced garlic, salt, and pepper. Drizzle over the quinoa mixture.
4. Toss everything gently to combine. Adjust seasoning as needed. Serve warm or chilled.

Nutritional Information: 280 calories, 8g protein, 30g carbohydrates, 15g fat, 4g fiber, 8mg cholesterol, 350mg sodium, 320mg potassium.

Instant Farro & Vegetable Medley

Yield: 4 servings | Prep time: 15 minutes | Cook time: 25 minutes

Ingredients:

- 1 cup farro, rinsed and drained
- 2 1/4 cups vegetable broth or water
- 1 medium zucchini, diced
- 1 red bell pepper, diced
- 1/2 cup cherry tomatoes, halved
- 1/4 cup red onion, finely chopped
- 3 tbsp olive oil
- 2 tbsp fresh basil, chopped
- 1 tbsp balsamic vinegar
- Salt and pepper to taste
- 1/4 cup grated Parmesan cheese (optional)
- 2 cloves garlic, minced

Directions:

1. In the Instant Pot, combine farro, vegetable broth (or water), zucchini, red bell pepper, cherry tomatoes, and red onion.
2. Secure the lid and set the pot to the "Manual" or "Pressure Cook" setting. Cook for 10 minutes at high pressure. Allow a natural release for 10 minutes, then perform a quick release.
3. In a small bowl, mix together olive oil, balsamic vinegar, minced garlic, salt, and pepper to create a dressing. Pour over the cooked farro and vegetable mixture in the Instant Pot.
4. Stir in fresh basil and adjust seasoning as desired. If using, sprinkle with Parmesan cheese before serving.

Nutritional Information: 320 calories, 10g protein, 50g carbohydrates, 11g fat, 8g fiber, 5mg cholesterol, 300mg sodium, 370mg potassium.

Couscous with Caramelized Onions

Yield: 4 servings | Prep time: 10 minutes | Cook time: 20 minutes

Ingredients:

- 1 1/2 cups couscous
- 2 large onions, thinly sliced
- 3 tbsp olive oil
- 2 cups vegetable broth or water
- 1/4 cup raisins or currants
- 1/4 cup slivered almonds, toasted
- 2 tbsp fresh parsley, finely chopped
- Salt and pepper to taste

Directions:

1. Set the Instant Pot to the "Sauté" function. Add olive oil and sliced onions. Sauté until the onions are deeply caramelized, about 15 minutes, stirring occasionally to prevent burning.
2. Pour in the vegetable broth or water and deglaze the bottom of the pot by scraping any browned bits with a wooden spoon.
3. Stir in the couscous, raisins, and toasted almonds. Secure the lid, set the pot to "Manual" or "Pressure Cook" setting, and adjust the time to 5 minutes at low pressure. Once done, quick release the pressure.
4. Fluff the couscous with a fork, then stir in chopped parsley. Season with salt and pepper as desired before serving.

Nutritional Information: 380 calories, 10g protein, 65g carbohydrates, 9g fat, 4g fiber, 0mg cholesterol, 220mg sodium, 320mg potassium.

Bulgur Wheat Pilaf with Herbs

Yield: 4 servings | Prep time: 10 minutes | Cook time: 12 minutes

Ingredients:

- 1 cup bulgur wheat
- 2 cups vegetable broth
- 1 medium onion, finely chopped
- 2 tbsp olive oil
- 1/4 cup fresh parsley, chopped
- 1/4 cup fresh mint, chopped
- 1/4 cup fresh dill, chopped
- 1 lemon, zested and juiced
- Salt and pepper to taste

Directions:

1. Set the Instant Pot to the "Sauté" function. Add olive oil and chopped onions. Sauté until the onions are translucent, about 3-4 minutes.
2. Add bulgur wheat to the pot and stir for another 2 minutes, allowing the grains to lightly toast.
3. Pour in the vegetable broth. Secure the lid, set the pot to the "Manual" or "Pressure Cook" setting, and adjust the time to 10 minutes on low pressure. Once done, allow the pressure to naturally release for 5 minutes, then quick release any remaining pressure.
4. Stir in parsley, mint, dill, lemon zest, and lemon juice. Adjust with salt and pepper as needed before serving.

Nutritional Information: 210 calories, 6g protein, 40g carbohydrates, 4g fat, 8g fiber, 0mg cholesterol, 150mg sodium, 280mg potassium.

Instant Pot Orzo with Lemon

Yield: 4 servings | Prep time: 5 minutes | Cook time: 7 minutes

Ingredients:

- 1 cup orzo pasta
- 2 cups vegetable broth
- Zest and juice of 1 lemon
- 2 tbsp olive oil
- 2 garlic cloves, minced
- 1/4 cup fresh parsley, finely chopped
- Salt and pepper to taste
- Optional: grated Parmesan cheese for serving

Directions:

1. Set the Instant Pot to the "Sauté" mode. Add olive oil and minced garlic. Sauté for about 1 minute until fragrant.
2. Add the orzo pasta and stir, coating the pasta in the garlic and oil for about 1 minute.
3. Pour in the vegetable broth and add the lemon zest. Secure the lid, set the pot to the "Manual" or "Pressure Cook" setting, and adjust to 4 minutes on high pressure.
4. Once the cooking cycle completes, quick release the pressure. Stir in the lemon juice, parsley, salt, and pepper. Serve with optional grated Parmesan on top.

Nutritional Information: 220 calories, 7g protein, 35g carbohydrates, 6g fat, 2g fiber, 0mg cholesterol, 450mg sodium, 100mg potassium.

Saffron Millet Delight

Yield: 4 servings | Prep time: 10 minutes | Cook time: 20 minutes

Ingredients:

- 1 cup millet, rinsed and drained
- 2 cups vegetable broth
- A pinch of saffron threads (around 20 threads), soaked in 2 tablespoons warm water
- 2 tbsp olive oil
- 1 onion, finely chopped
- 2 garlic cloves, minced
- 1/2 cup green peas
- 1/2 cup diced carrots
- 1/4 cup fresh parsley, finely chopped
- Salt and pepper to taste
- Zest of 1 lemon

Directions:

1. Set the Instant Pot to the "Sauté" mode. Add olive oil, chopped onion, and minced garlic. Sauté until translucent.
2. Add millet to the pot, stirring for 2 minutes to toast slightly.
3. Pour in the vegetable broth, add the peas, carrots, and saffron along with its soaking water. Stir everything well.
4. Secure the lid, set the pot to the "Manual" or "Pressure Cook" setting, and adjust to 15 minutes on high pressure.
5. Once the cooking cycle completes, allow for a natural release for 5 minutes and then perform a quick release. Stir in the lemon zest, parsley, salt, and pepper before serving.

Nutritional Information: 280 calories, 7g protein, 48g carbohydrates, 7g fat, 5g fiber, 0mg cholesterol, 520mg sodium, 230mg potassium.

Barley & Vegetable Risotto
Yield: 4 servings | Prep time: 15 minutes | Cook time: 25 minutes

Ingredients:

- 1 cup pearl barley, rinsed and drained
- 2 1/2 cups vegetable broth
- 2 tbsp olive oil
- 1 medium onion, diced
- 2 cloves garlic, minced
- 1 bell pepper, diced (color of your choice)
- 1 zucchini, diced
- 1/2 cup cherry tomatoes, halved
- 1/4 cup grated Parmesan cheese (optional for dairy-free/vegan)
- 1/4 cup fresh basil, chopped
- Salt and pepper to taste

Directions:

1. Set the Instant Pot to "Sauté" mode. Add olive oil, diced onion, and minced garlic. Cook until the onions are translucent.
2. Add the bell pepper and zucchini, and sauté for another 2-3 minutes.
3. Stir in the pearl barley, ensuring it's well-mixed with the vegetables. Pour in the vegetable broth.
4. Secure the Instant Pot lid, set to "Manual" or "Pressure Cook" mode, and adjust the time to 20 minutes on high pressure.
5. Once cooking completes, allow for a natural release for 10 minutes and then do a quick release. Stir in the cherry tomatoes, grated Parmesan (if using), fresh basil, salt, and pepper. Serve while hot.
6. **Nutritional Information:** 270 calories, 8g protein, 48g carbohydrates, 7g fat, 9g fiber, 5mg cholesterol, 550mg sodium, 320mg potassium.

Express Mediterranean Rice
Yield: 4 servings | Prep time: 10 minutes | Cook time: 20 minutes

Ingredients:

- 1 1/2 cups long-grain white rice, rinsed
- 2 cups vegetable broth
- 1 tbsp olive oil
- 1 small onion, finely chopped
- 2 cloves garlic, minced
- 1/2 cup cherry tomatoes, halved
- 1/3 cup Kalamata olives, pitted and sliced
- 1/4 cup fresh parsley, chopped
- Zest and juice of 1 lemon
- Salt and pepper to taste
- 1/4 cup crumbled feta cheese (optional)

Directions:

1. Set the Instant Pot to "Sauté" mode. Add olive oil, chopped onion, and minced garlic. Cook until the onions are translucent.
2. Add rice and stir, ensuring it's well-coated with the oil and onions.
3. Pour in the vegetable broth. Secure the Instant Pot lid, set to "Manual" or "Pressure Cook" mode, and adjust the time to 12 minutes on high pressure.
4. Once cooking completes, allow for a natural release for 5 minutes and then do a quick release. Stir in the cherry tomatoes, olives, parsley, lemon zest, lemon juice, salt, and pepper. Top with crumbled feta if desired before serving.

Nutritional Information: 350 calories, 7g protein, 65g carbohydrates, 6g fat, 3g fiber, 10mg cholesterol, 500mg sodium, 280mg potassium.

Moroccan Spiced Freekeh

Yield: 4 servings | Prep time: 15 minutes | Cook time: 25 minutes

Ingredients:

- 1 cup freekeh, rinsed and drained
- 2 1/2 cups vegetable broth
- 1 tbsp olive oil
- 1 medium onion, finely chopped
- 2 cloves garlic, minced
- 1/2 cup dried apricots, chopped
- 1/4 cup slivered almonds
- 1 tsp ground cumin
- 1/2 tsp ground cinnamon
- 1/4 tsp ground coriander
- 1/4 tsp ground turmeric
- Salt and pepper to taste
- 2 tbsp fresh cilantro, chopped

Directions:

1. Set the Instant Pot to "Sauté" mode. Add olive oil, chopped onion, and minced garlic. Cook until the onions are translucent.
2. Stir in the spices (cumin, cinnamon, coriander, and turmeric), allowing them to toast for about 1 minute.
3. Add the rinsed freekeh to the pot and stir to coat with the onion-spice mixture. Pour in the vegetable broth.
4. Close the Instant Pot lid, set it to "Manual" or "Pressure Cook" mode, and adjust the time to 20 minutes on high pressure.
5. Once cooking completes, allow a natural release for 10 minutes and then do a quick release. Stir in dried apricots, almonds, and cilantro. Season with salt and pepper to taste.

Nutritional Information: 320 calories, 9g protein, 55g carbohydrates, 8g fat, 8g fiber, 0mg cholesterol, 480mg sodium, 320mg potassium.

Herb-Infused Sorghum

Yield: 4 servings | Prep time: 10 minutes | Cook time: 30 minutes

Ingredients:

- 1 cup sorghum grains, rinsed and drained
- 2 1/2 cups vegetable broth
- 1 tbsp olive oil
- 2 cloves garlic, minced
- 1 bay leaf
- 1 sprig rosemary
- 1 sprig thyme
- Salt and pepper to taste
- 1/4 cup fresh parsley, chopped
- Zest of 1 lemon

Directions:

1. Set the Instant Pot to "Sauté" mode. Add olive oil and minced garlic. Cook until garlic is aromatic but not browned.
2. Add the rinsed sorghum grains to the pot, stirring to coat them in the oil and garlic.
3. Pour in the vegetable broth, then add the bay leaf, rosemary, and thyme sprigs.
4. Close the Instant Pot lid, set it to "Manual" or "Pressure Cook" mode, and adjust the time to 25 minutes on high pressure.
5. Once cooking completes, allow a natural release for 10 minutes before performing a quick release. Discard the bay leaf and herb sprigs. Stir in fresh parsley and lemon zest. Season with salt and pepper to taste.

Nutritional Information: 240 calories, 6g protein, 49g carbohydrates, 4g fat, 5g fiber, 0mg cholesterol, 480mg sodium, 290mg potassium.

Vegetable Delights

Stuffed Eggplants with Rice

Yield: 4 servings | Prep time: 15 minutes | Cook time: 20 minutes

Ingredients:

- 2 medium eggplants, halved lengthwise
- 1 cup long-grain rice, rinsed and drained
- 2 tbsp olive oil
- 1 onion, finely chopped
- 2 cloves garlic, minced
- 1 tomato, diced
- 1/4 cup fresh parsley, chopped
- 1/4 cup fresh mint, chopped
- 1/2 tsp ground cumin
- 1 tsp paprika
- Salt and pepper to taste
- 2 cups vegetable broth
- Juice of half a lemon
- 1/4 cup pine nuts or slivered almonds (optional for garnish)

Directions:

1. Scoop out the center of each eggplant half, leaving about a half-inch border. Chop the scooped-out eggplant flesh. Set the Instant Pot to "Sauté" mode. Add olive oil, onion, and garlic. Sauté until onion is translucent. Add chopped eggplant, tomatoes, rice, cumin, paprika, and half of the parsley and mint. Stir well for about 2-3 minutes.
2. Fill each eggplant half with the rice mixture and place them side by side in the Instant Pot. Pour vegetable broth and lemon juice over the stuffed eggplants.
3. Close the Instant Pot lid, set it to "Manual" or "Pressure Cook" mode, and adjust the time to 15 minutes on high pressure. Once cooking completes, allow a natural release. Garnish with remaining parsley, mint, and optionally, pine nuts or almonds.

Nutritional Information: 350 calories, 8g protein, 60g carbohydrates, 10g fat, 9g fiber, 0mg cholesterol, 600mg sodium, 790mg potassium.

Mediterranean Vegetable Curry

Yield: 4 servings | Prep time: 20 minutes | Cook time: 15 minutes

Ingredients:

- 2 tbsp olive oil
- 1 large onion, finely chopped
- 3 cloves garlic, minced
- 1 bell pepper (red or yellow), diced
- 1 zucchini, diced
- 1 eggplant, diced
- 2 tomatoes, chopped
- 2 cups chickpeas, rinsed and drained
- 1 cup coconut milk
- 2 tsp ground turmeric
- 1 tsp ground cumin
- 1 tsp smoked paprika
- 1/2 tsp chili flakes (adjust for heat preference)
- Salt and pepper to taste
- 2 tbsp fresh cilantro, chopped (for garnish)
- Juice of 1 lemon

Directions:

1. Set the Instant Pot to "Sauté" mode. Add olive oil, onion, and garlic. Sauté until the onion is translucent.
2. Add bell pepper, zucchini, eggplant, tomatoes, and spices (turmeric, cumin, paprika, chili flakes, salt, and pepper). Stir well. Add chickpeas and coconut milk, ensuring the vegetables are submerged.
3. Close the Instant Pot lid, set it to "Manual" or "Pressure Cook" mode, and adjust the time to 10 minutes on high pressure.
4. Once cooking completes, quick release the pressure. Stir in lemon juice, taste for seasoning adjustments, and garnish with fresh cilantro before serving.

Nutritional Information: 310 calories, 9g protein, 45g carbohydrates, 12g fat, 12g fiber, 0mg cholesterol, 320mg sodium, 820mg potassium.

Instant Ratatouille

Yield: 4 servings | Prep time: 15 minutes | Cook time: 8 minutes

Ingredients:

- 2 tbsp olive oil
- 1 large onion, sliced
- 3 cloves garlic, minced
- 1 bell pepper (red or yellow), sliced
- 1 zucchini, sliced
- 1 eggplant, diced
- 2 tomatoes, chopped
- 1/2 cup vegetable broth
- 2 tsp dried basil
- 1 tsp dried thyme
- Salt and pepper to taste
- 2 tbsp fresh basil, chopped (for garnish)
- Grated parmesan cheese (optional, for serving)

Directions:

1. Set the Instant Pot to "Sauté" mode. Add olive oil, onion, and garlic. Sauté for 2-3 minutes until the onion starts to become translucent.
2. Add bell pepper, zucchini, eggplant, tomatoes, dried basil, dried thyme, salt, and pepper. Stir well.
3. Pour in vegetable broth.
4. Close the Instant Pot lid, set it to "Manual" or "Pressure Cook" mode, and adjust the time to 5 minutes on high pressure.
5. Once cooking completes, quick release the pressure. Garnish with fresh basil and optionally serve with grated parmesan cheese.

Nutritional Information: 140 calories, 3g protein, 25g carbohydrates, 5g fat, 7g fiber, 0mg cholesterol, 230mg sodium, 700mg potassium.

Zucchini & Tomato Medley

Yield: 4 servings | Prep time: 10 minutes | Cook time: 4 minutes

Ingredients:

- 2 tbsp olive oil
- 1 medium onion, finely chopped
- 3 cloves garlic, minced
- 3 medium zucchinis, sliced
- 2 cups cherry tomatoes, halved
- 1/2 tsp dried basil
- 1/2 tsp dried oregano
- Salt and pepper to taste
- 2 tbsp fresh parsley, chopped
- 1/4 cup feta cheese crumbles (optional)

Directions:

1. Set the Instant Pot to "Sauté" mode. Add olive oil, onion, and garlic. Sauté for 2 minutes until the onion is translucent.
2. Add zucchinis, cherry tomatoes, dried basil, dried oregano, salt, and pepper. Stir to combine.
3. Close the Instant Pot lid, set it to "Manual" or "Pressure Cook" mode, and adjust the time to 2 minutes on high pressure.
4. Once cooking completes, quick release the pressure. Gently stir in fresh parsley and top with feta cheese crumbles if desired before serving.

Nutritional Information: 120 calories, 3g protein, 11g carbohydrates, 8g fat, 3g fiber, 8mg cholesterol, 150mg sodium, 480mg potassium.

Artichoke & Lemon Stew

Yield: 4 servings | Prep time: 15 minutes | Cook time: 25 minutes

Ingredients:

- 2 tbsp olive oil
- 1 onion, finely chopped
- 3 cloves garlic, minced
- 8 fresh artichokes, cleaned, trimmed, and quartered
- Zest and juice of 2 lemons
- 2 cups vegetable broth
- 1/2 cup white wine (optional)
- 2 bay leaves
- 1 tsp dried thyme
- Salt and pepper to taste
- 2 tbsp fresh parsley, chopped (for garnish)

Directions:

1. Set the Instant Pot to "Sauté" mode. Add olive oil, onion, and garlic. Sauté for 3 minutes until the onion becomes translucent.
2. Add artichokes, lemon zest, lemon juice, vegetable broth, white wine (if using), bay leaves, dried thyme, salt, and pepper to the pot. Stir to combine.
3. Secure the Instant Pot lid, set it to "Manual" or "Pressure Cook" mode, and adjust the time to 20 minutes on high pressure.
4. Once the cooking completes, let the pressure release naturally for 5 minutes and then quick release any remaining pressure. Discard the bay leaves and garnish with fresh parsley before serving.

Nutritional Information: 180 calories, 5g protein, 30g carbohydrates, 7g fat, 10g fiber, 0mg cholesterol, 450mg sodium, 800mg potassium.

Roasted Red Pepper Soup

Yield: 4 servings | Prep time: 10 minutes | Cook time: 20 minutes

Ingredients:

- 4 large red bell peppers, seeded and quartered
- 1 tbsp olive oil
- 1 medium onion, chopped
- 3 cloves garlic, minced
- 1 carrot, chopped
- 4 cups vegetable broth
- 1 tsp smoked paprika
- 1/2 tsp ground cumin
- 1/2 cup coconut milk or Greek yogurt (optional for creaminess)
- Salt and pepper to taste
- Fresh basil or parsley, for garnish

Directions:

1. Set the Instant Pot to "Sauté" mode. Add olive oil, onion, garlic, and carrot. Sauté for 4-5 minutes until the onion becomes translucent.
2. Add roasted red bell peppers, vegetable broth, smoked paprika, cumin, salt, and pepper to the pot. Stir to combine.
3. Secure the Instant Pot lid, set it to "Manual" or "Pressure Cook" mode, and adjust the time to 15 minutes on high pressure.
4. Once the cooking completes, let the pressure release naturally. Use an immersion blender to puree the soup to your desired consistency. Stir in coconut milk or Greek yogurt, if using. Taste and adjust seasoning if needed.

Nutritional Information: 120 calories, 3g protein, 18g carbohydrates, 5g fat, 5g fiber, 0mg cholesterol, 300mg sodium, 500mg potassium.

Spinach & Feta Stuffed Tomatoes

Yield: 4 servings | Prep time: 15 minutes | Cook time: 10 minutes

Ingredients:

- 4 large tomatoes, tops removed and hollowed out
- 2 cups fresh spinach, chopped
- 1 cup feta cheese, crumbled
- 1 tbsp olive oil
- 2 cloves garlic, minced
- 1 small onion, finely chopped
- 1/4 tsp black pepper
- 1/4 tsp dried oregano
- 1/4 cup fresh parsley, chopped
- 1/2 cup water (for Instant Pot)

Directions:

1. On "Sauté" mode, heat olive oil in the Instant Pot. Add garlic and onion. Sauté until onion is translucent, about 2-3 minutes.
2. Add spinach, black pepper, and oregano to the pot. Sauté until spinach is wilted, approximately 2 minutes. Turn off the pot and let the mixture cool slightly. Stir in feta cheese and fresh parsley.
3. Stuff each tomato with the spinach and feta mixture.
4. Pour water into the Instant Pot, then place the stuffed tomatoes on the trivet or steam rack inside. Secure the lid and set the pot to "Manual" or "Pressure Cook" for 5 minutes on low pressure.
5. Quick release the pressure and carefully remove the tomatoes using a pair of tongs.

Nutritional Information: 140 calories, 6g protein, 11g carbohydrates, 8g fat, 3g fiber, 25mg cholesterol, 350mg sodium, 400mg potassium.

Pressure-Cooked Mediterranean Veggie Mix

Yield: 4 servings | Prep time: 10 minutes | Cook time: 5 minutes

Ingredients:

- 1 medium zucchini, sliced
- 1 red bell pepper, chopped
- 1 yellow bell pepper, chopped
- 1 small eggplant, diced
- 1 cup cherry tomatoes, halved
- 1/4 cup kalamata olives, pitted and sliced
- 3 tbsp olive oil
- 2 cloves garlic, minced
- 1 tsp dried basil
- 1 tsp dried oregano
- 1/4 cup feta cheese, crumbled (optional)
- Salt and pepper, to taste
- 1/2 cup water (for Instant Pot)

Directions:

1. In a mixing bowl, combine zucchini, bell peppers, eggplant, cherry tomatoes, and olives. Drizzle with olive oil, sprinkle with garlic, basil, oregano, salt, and pepper. Toss to coat.
2. Add water to the Instant Pot. Place the vegetable mixture in a steamer basket or on a trivet inside the pot.
3. Secure the lid and set the pot to "Manual" or "Pressure Cook" for 5 minutes on high pressure.
4. Perform a quick release of the pressure. Transfer the vegetables to a serving dish and if desired, sprinkle with crumbled feta cheese before serving.

Nutritional Information: 180 calories, 4g protein, 15g carbohydrates, 12g fat, 5g fiber, 8mg cholesterol, 220mg sodium, 600mg potassium.

Olive & Capers Veggie Toss

Yield: 4 servings | Prep time: 15 minutes | Cook time: 4 minutes

Ingredients:

- 1 cup green olives, pitted and sliced
- 3 tbsp capers, drained
- 2 large zucchinis, sliced
- 1 red bell pepper, chopped
- 1 yellow bell pepper, chopped
- 2 tbsp olive oil
- 2 cloves garlic, minced
- 1 tsp dried rosemary
- 1/4 cup fresh parsley, chopped
- Salt and black pepper, to taste
- 1/2 cup water (for Instant Pot)

Directions:

1. In a bowl, combine olives, capers, zucchinis, and bell peppers. Drizzle with olive oil, add garlic, rosemary, salt, and pepper. Toss to coat the vegetables well.
2. Add water to the Instant Pot. Place the vegetable mixture into the pot.
3. Secure the lid and set the pot to "Manual" or "Pressure Cook" for 4 minutes on high pressure.
4. Once done, perform a quick release of the pressure. Transfer the vegetables to a serving dish and garnish with fresh parsley before serving.

Nutritional Information: 140 calories, 2g protein, 10g carbohydrates, 10g fat, 4g fiber, 0mg cholesterol, 420mg sodium, 400mg potassium.

Potato & Green Beans in Tomato Sauce

Yield: 4 servings | Prep time: 20 minutes | Cook time: 15 minutes

Ingredients:

- 4 medium potatoes, peeled and diced
- 2 cups fresh green beans, trimmed and cut into 2-inch lengths
- 1 can (28 oz) diced tomatoes
- 2 tbsp olive oil
- 1 onion, finely chopped
- 3 garlic cloves, minced
- 1 tsp dried oregano
- 1/2 tsp dried basil
- Salt and black pepper, to taste
- 1/2 cup water (for Instant Pot)
- Fresh parsley, chopped for garnish

Directions:

1. In the Instant Pot, select the "Sauté" setting and add olive oil. Once hot, add the chopped onions and garlic. Sauté until the onions become translucent.
2. Add the diced tomatoes (with juice), oregano, basil, salt, and pepper. Stir well.
3. Add the diced potatoes and green beans, mixing gently. Pour in the water.
4. Close the lid and set the Instant Pot to "Manual" or "Pressure Cook" for 15 minutes on high pressure. Once cooking is complete, perform a quick release of pressure.
5. Open the lid, stir gently, and transfer to serving dishes. Garnish with fresh parsley before serving.

Nutritional Information: 250 calories, 5g protein, 45g carbohydrates, 7g fat, 9g fiber, 0mg cholesterol, 250mg sodium, 950mg potassium.

Seafood Sensations

Quick Seafood Paella

Yield: 4 servings | Prep time: 20 minutes | Cook time: 10 minutes

Ingredients:

- 1 cup Arborio or short-grain rice, rinsed
- 1 1/2 cups chicken or vegetable broth
- 1/2 lb shrimp, peeled and deveined
- 1/2 lb mussels, cleaned and debearded
- 1/2 lb calamari rings
- 1 onion, finely chopped
- 2 garlic cloves, minced
- 1 bell pepper, chopped
- 1/2 cup frozen peas
- 1/4 cup olive oil
- 1 tsp smoked paprika
- 1 tsp saffron threads
- Salt and pepper, to taste
- 2 tomatoes, diced
- 2 tbsp fresh parsley, chopped
- 1 lemon, sliced for garnish

Directions:

1. Turn on the Instant Pot and select the "Sauté" setting. Add olive oil, onions, bell pepper, and garlic. Sauté until onions become translucent.
2. Add rice, paprika, saffron, salt, and pepper. Stir well to coat the rice in the seasonings and oil.
3. Pour in the broth, followed by the seafood, peas, and tomatoes. Stir gently to combine.
4. Secure the Instant Pot lid and set to "Manual" or "Pressure Cook" on high pressure for 10 minutes. Once finished, perform a quick release.
5. Serve the paella in bowls, garnished with fresh parsley and lemon slices.

Nutritional Information: 410 calories, 29g protein, 49g carbohydrates, 12g fat, 3g fiber, 130mg cholesterol, 620mg sodium, 570mg potassium.

Instant Pot Shrimp Scampi

Yield: 4 servings | Prep time: 10 minutes | Cook time: 5 minutes

Ingredients:

- 1 lb large shrimp, peeled and deveined
- 8 oz linguine or spaghetti
- 4 cloves garlic, minced
- 2 tbsp olive oil
- 1/4 cup dry white wine (or chicken broth)
- 1/2 cup chicken broth
- Zest and juice of 1 lemon
- 1 tsp red pepper flakes (optional for heat)
- Salt and pepper, to taste
- 1/4 cup fresh parsley, chopped
- 2 tbsp unsalted butter

Directions:

1. Turn the Instant Pot on the "Sauté" setting. Add olive oil and garlic, sautéing until fragrant.
2. Add white wine to deglaze, scraping the bottom of the pot. Then add in the chicken broth, lemon zest, lemon juice, red pepper flakes, salt, and pepper. Break the pasta in half and add to the pot, ensuring it's submerged in the liquid.
3. Secure the lid and set the Instant Pot to "Manual" or "Pressure Cook" on high pressure for 5 minutes. Once completed, do a quick release.
4. Turn back to "Sauté" mode. Stir in the shrimp, cooking until they turn pink. Finish with butter and parsley, stirring until the butter melts into the sauce.
5. Serve immediately, garnishing with additional parsley if desired.

Nutritional Information: 380 calories, 28g protein, 41g carbohydrates, 10g fat, 2g fiber, 180mg cholesterol, 570mg sodium, 370mg potassium.

Lemon Herb Fish Fillets

Yield: 4 servings | Prep time: 10 minutes | Cook time: 5 minutes

Ingredients:

- 4 fish fillets (such as cod, tilapia, or halibut)
- 2 cups water
- 1 lemon, thinly sliced
- 2 cloves garlic, minced
- 2 tbsp olive oil
- 2 tbsp fresh parsley, chopped
- 2 tsp fresh thyme leaves
- 1 tsp fresh rosemary, chopped
- Salt and pepper, to taste

Directions:

1. In the Instant Pot, add water, then place the trivet or a steaming basket inside.
2. Season the fish fillets with salt, pepper, and garlic. Place them on the trivet or in the steaming basket.
3. Drizzle olive oil over the fish. Place the lemon slices and sprinkle the herbs evenly over the fillets.
4. Secure the Instant Pot lid and set the valve to "Sealing". Choose the "Steam" function and set the timer for 5 minutes. Once the cooking is done, quickly release the pressure.
5. Carefully open the lid, remove the fish fillets, and serve immediately.

Nutritional Information: 220 calories, 28g protein, 3g carbohydrates, 10g fat, 1g fiber, 85mg cholesterol, 320mg sodium, 470mg potassium.

Pressure-Cooked Mussels in White Wine

Yield: 4 servings | Prep time: 15 minutes | Cook time: 2 minutes

Ingredients:

- 2 pounds fresh mussels, cleaned and debearded
- 1 cup dry white wine (such as Sauvignon Blanc)
- 4 cloves garlic, minced
- 1 small onion, finely chopped
- 2 tablespoons olive oil
- 1/4 cup fresh parsley, chopped
- Zest of 1 lemon
- Salt and pepper, to taste
- 1 pinch red pepper flakes (optional)

Directions:

1. Turn on the Instant Pot's sauté function and add olive oil. Once hot, sauté garlic and onion until translucent.
2. Add mussels to the pot followed by white wine, lemon zest, salt, pepper, and red pepper flakes (if using). Give a gentle stir.
3. Close and seal the Instant Pot. Set to manual high pressure for 2 minutes.
4. After cooking, do a quick pressure release. Open the lid and discard any mussels that haven't opened. Stir in fresh parsley.
5. Serve the mussels hot with a bit of the broth in bowls.

Nutritional Information: 250 calories, 18g protein, 10g carbohydrates, 8g fat, 0.5g fiber, 50mg cholesterol, 480mg sodium, 450mg potassium.

Mediterranean Octopus Salad

Yield: 4 servings | Prep time: 20 minutes | Cook time: 25 minutes

Ingredients:

- 1 pound octopus tentacles, cleaned
- 2 cups water
- 1 bay leaf
- 1 teaspoon sea salt
- 1/4 cup extra-virgin olive oil
- 2 tablespoons lemon juice
- 1 tablespoon red wine vinegar
- 1/2 cup cherry tomatoes, halved
- 1/4 cup red onion, thinly sliced
- 1/4 cup Kalamata olives, pitted
- 1/4 cup cucumber, diced
- 2 tablespoons fresh parsley, chopped
- 1 tablespoon fresh oregano, chopped
- Freshly ground black pepper, to taste

Directions:

1. In the Instant Pot, combine the water, bay leaf, and sea salt. Add the octopus tentacles. Close the lid and set the pot to manual high pressure for 25 minutes.
2. Once cooking is complete, release pressure naturally. Remove the octopus and let it cool. Slice the tentacles into bite-sized pieces.
3. In a large bowl, combine the octopus slices, cherry tomatoes, red onion, olives, and cucumber.
4. Whisk together the olive oil, lemon juice, red wine vinegar, parsley, oregano, salt, and black pepper. Pour over the salad and toss to combine.
5. Serve the salad chilled or at room temperature.

Nutritional Information: 220 calories, 18g protein, 8g carbohydrates, 12g fat, 2g fiber, 50mg cholesterol, 420mg sodium, 500mg potassium.

Clams in Spicy Tomato Sauce

Yield: 4 servings | Prep time: 15 minutes | Cook time: 10 minutes

Ingredients:

- 2 pounds fresh clams, cleaned and scrubbed
- 1 tablespoon extra-virgin olive oil
- 4 garlic cloves, minced
- 1 small red chili pepper, finely chopped (adjust to desired heat level)
- 1 cup tomato sauce (preferably homemade or low-sodium store-bought)
- 1/4 cup white wine
- 2 tablespoons fresh parsley, chopped
- Zest and juice of 1 lemon
- Salt and freshly ground black pepper, to taste

Directions:

1. Set the Instant Pot to sauté mode and heat the olive oil. Add garlic and red chili pepper, sautéing for about 2 minutes until fragrant.
2. Pour in the white wine, allowing it to simmer and reduce by half.
3. Add the tomato sauce and mix well. Place the cleaned clams into the pot, stirring to coat them with the sauce.
4. Close the Instant Pot lid, set to manual high pressure for 5 minutes. Once done, quick release the pressure. Discard any clams that did not open.
5. Stir in lemon zest, juice, and fresh parsley. Season with salt and black pepper. Serve hot.

Nutritional Information: 150 calories, 14g protein, 10g carbohydrates, 4g fat, 1g fiber, 40mg cholesterol, 380mg sodium, 400mg potassium.

Olive Oil & Garlic Braised Calamari

Yield: 4 servings | Prep time: 10 minutes | Cook time: 20 minutes

Ingredients:

- 1.5 pounds of calamari, cleaned and sliced into rings
- 4 tablespoons extra-virgin olive oil
- 6 garlic cloves, thinly sliced
- 1/2 cup white wine
- 1/4 cup fresh parsley, chopped
- Zest and juice of 1 lemon
- Salt and freshly ground black pepper, to taste
- Red chili flakes (optional, for added heat)

Directions:

1. Set the Instant Pot to sauté mode. Add the olive oil and sliced garlic. Sauté until the garlic becomes aromatic but not browned, about 2-3 minutes.
2. Add the calamari rings, stirring to ensure they are coated with the olive oil and garlic.
3. Pour in the white wine, allowing it to simmer for 2 minutes.
4. Close the Instant Pot lid and set it to manual low pressure for 15 minutes. After cooking, quick release the pressure.
5. Stir in the lemon zest, juice, parsley, and season with salt, black pepper, and chili flakes if using. Serve immediately.

Nutritional Information: 260 calories, 25g protein, 6g carbohydrates, 13g fat, 0.5g fiber, 375mg cholesterol, 100mg sodium, 350mg potassium.

Instant Tuna & Caper Stew

Yield: 4 servings | Prep time: 15 minutes | Cook time: 20 minutes

Ingredients:

- 2 cans (5 oz each) tuna in olive oil, drained
- 2 tablespoons extra-virgin olive oil
- 1 medium onion, finely chopped
- 3 cloves garlic, minced
- 1/4 cup capers, drained and rinsed
- 1 can (14 oz) diced tomatoes
- 1 cup vegetable broth
- 1/2 cup green olives, pitted and halved
- 2 tablespoons fresh parsley, chopped
- Zest and juice of 1 lemon
- Salt and freshly ground black pepper, to taste
- Red chili flakes (optional, for added heat)

Directions:

1. Set the Instant Pot to sauté mode. Add the olive oil, onion, and garlic. Sauté until onion is translucent, about 3-4 minutes.
2. Stir in the capers, tuna, and diced tomatoes.
3. Add the vegetable broth, olives, and lemon zest. Mix well.
4. Seal the Instant Pot and set to manual high pressure for 10 minutes. Once done, quick release the pressure.
5. Stir in the lemon juice and parsley. Season with salt, black pepper, and optional chili flakes. Serve warm.

Nutritional Information: 250 calories, 20g protein, 12g carbohydrates, 14g fat, 3g fiber, 35mg cholesterol, 720mg sodium, 450mg potassium.

Fish Tagine with Olives

Yield: 4 servings | Prep time: 20 minutes | Cook time: 15 minutes

Ingredients:

- 4 fish fillets (such as cod or haddock), about 6 ounces each
- 2 tablespoons extra-virgin olive oil
- 1 large onion, thinly sliced
- 3 cloves garlic, minced
- 1 teaspoon ground cumin
- 1 teaspoon ground paprika
- 1/2 teaspoon ground turmeric
- 1/4 teaspoon cayenne pepper (optional)
- 1 cup green olives, pitted
- 1 can (14 oz) diced tomatoes
- 1/2 cup vegetable broth or fish stock
- 2 tablespoons fresh cilantro, chopped
- 2 tablespoons fresh parsley, chopped
- Juice of 1 lemon
- Salt and pepper to taste

Directions:

1. Set the Instant Pot to sauté mode. Add olive oil, onion, and garlic. Sauté until onion becomes translucent, about 3-4 minutes. Add cumin, paprika, turmeric, and cayenne pepper, stirring for an additional minute.
2. Pour in the diced tomatoes, vegetable broth or fish stock, and add olives. Mix well.
3. Nestle the fish fillets into the mixture in the pot.
4. Seal the Instant Pot and set to manual high pressure for 7 minutes. Once cooking is complete, use a quick release.
5. Stir in fresh cilantro, parsley, and lemon juice. Adjust seasoning with salt and pepper as needed. Serve warm.

Nutritional Information: 280 calories, 30g protein, 15g carbohydrates, 11g fat, 4g fiber, 70mg cholesterol, 720mg sodium, 500mg potassium.

Quick Seafood Risotto

Yield: 4 servings | Prep time: 15 minutes | Cook time: 20 minutes

Ingredients:

- 1 tablespoon extra-virgin olive oil
- 1 small onion, finely chopped
- 2 cloves garlic, minced
- 1 cup Arborio rice
- 3 cups seafood stock or vegetable broth
- 1/2 cup white wine (optional)
- 1 cup mixed seafood (like shrimp, mussels, and calamari), cleaned and prepped
- 1/2 cup frozen peas, thawed
- 1/2 cup grated Parmesan cheese
- Zest and juice of 1 lemon
- 2 tablespoons fresh parsley, chopped
- Salt and pepper to taste

Directions:

1. Set the Instant Pot to sauté mode. Add olive oil, onion, and garlic. Sauté until the onion is translucent, about 3 minutes. Add the Arborio rice and cook, stirring, for an additional 2 minutes.
2. Pour in the white wine, if using, and allow it to evaporate slightly. Add the seafood stock or vegetable broth.
3. Seal the Instant Pot and set it to manual high pressure for 6 minutes. Once the cooking is complete, use a quick release.
4. Switch back to sauté mode. Add the mixed seafood and peas, stirring occasionally, until the seafood is cooked through, about 4-5 minutes. Stir in the Parmesan cheese, lemon zest, lemon juice, and parsley. Season with salt and pepper to taste before serving.

Nutritional Information: 380 calories, 20g protein, 55g carbohydrates, 7g fat, 2g fiber, 90mg cholesterol, 700mg sodium, 300mg potassium.

Poultry & Meats

Chicken Tagine with Preserved Lemons

Yield: 4 servings | Prep time: 20 minutes | Cook time: 25 minutes

Ingredients:

- 4 chicken thighs, bone-in and skin-on
- 2 tablespoons extra-virgin olive oil
- 1 large onion, thinly sliced
- 3 cloves garlic, minced
- 1 teaspoon ground cumin
- 1 teaspoon ground ginger
- 1 teaspoon ground turmeric
- 1/2 teaspoon ground cinnamon
- 1/4 teaspoon saffron threads, optional
- 1 cup chicken broth
- 2 preserved lemons, seeds removed and thinly sliced
- 1 cup green olives, pitted
- 2 tablespoons fresh cilantro, chopped
- Salt and pepper, to taste

Directions:

1. On the sauté setting, heat the olive oil in the Instant Pot. Season the chicken thighs with salt and pepper, then brown them on both sides. Remove and set aside.
2. In the same pot, add onions and garlic, sautéing until translucent. Stir in cumin, ginger, turmeric, cinnamon, and saffron threads, allowing the spices to toast briefly.
3. Return the browned chicken to the pot and add chicken broth, preserved lemons, and olives. Seal the Instant Pot lid and set to manual high pressure for 20 minutes. Once cooking is complete, use a natural release.
4. Before serving, stir in fresh cilantro and adjust seasonings if necessary.

Nutritional Information: 380 calories, 28g protein, 12g carbohydrates, 24g fat, 3g fiber, 110mg cholesterol, 850mg sodium, 450mg potassium.

Lamb Shanks in Tomato Sauce

Yield: 4 servings | Prep time: 15 minutes | Cook time: 45 minutes

Ingredients:

- 4 lamb shanks, trimmed
- 2 tablespoons extra-virgin olive oil
- 1 large onion, chopped
- 3 cloves garlic, minced
- 1 cup dry red wine
- 2 cups canned diced tomatoes
- 2 sprigs fresh rosemary
- 2 sprigs fresh thyme
- 1 bay leaf
- Salt and freshly ground black pepper, to taste
- Zest of 1 lemon
- 2 tablespoons fresh parsley, chopped (for garnish)

Directions:

1. On the sauté setting, heat olive oil in the Instant Pot. Season lamb shanks with salt and pepper, then sear them on all sides until browned. Remove and set aside.
2. In the same pot, add onions and garlic, sautéing until translucent. Pour in the wine, stirring and scraping up any browned bits from the bottom of the pot.
3. Add diced tomatoes, rosemary, thyme, bay leaf, and lemon zest. Return the browned lamb shanks to the pot, nestling them in the sauce.
4. Seal the Instant Pot lid and set to manual high pressure for 40 minutes. Once cooking is complete, use a natural release for 10 minutes, then release any remaining pressure.
5. Before serving, garnish with fresh parsley.

Nutritional Information: 490 calories, 38g protein, 15g carbohydrates, 24g fat, 3g fiber, 140mg cholesterol, 550mg sodium, 760mg potassium.

Pressure-Cooked Beef Gyros

Yield: 4 servings | Prep time: 20 minutes | Cook time: 50 minutes

Ingredients:

- 1.5 lbs beef roast, sliced thinly
- 2 tablespoons extra-virgin olive oil
- 1 large onion, thinly sliced
- 4 cloves garlic, minced
- 1 cup beef broth
- 2 teaspoons dried oregano
- 1 teaspoon dried rosemary
- Salt and freshly ground black pepper, to taste
- 4 pita breads
- 1 cup Greek yogurt (for serving)
- 1 cucumber, diced (for serving)
- 2 tomatoes, diced (for serving)
- 1/2 cup feta cheese, crumbled (for serving)

Directions:

1. On the sauté setting, heat olive oil in the Instant Pot. Add beef slices and brown them lightly on both sides. Remove and set aside.
2. Add onions and garlic to the pot, sautéing until translucent.
3. Return the beef to the pot and add beef broth, oregano, rosemary, salt, and pepper. Mix well to combine.
4. Secure the Instant Pot lid and set to manual high pressure for 45 minutes. Once cooking is complete, use a natural release for 5 minutes, then release any remaining pressure.
5. Serve beef slices in pita breads, topped with Greek yogurt, cucumber, tomatoes, and feta cheese.

Nutritional Information: 560 calories, 40g protein, 40g carbohydrates, 25g fat, 5g fiber, 105mg cholesterol, 700mg sodium, 680mg potassium.

Instant Pot Herb-Roasted Chicken

Yield: 4 servings | Prep time: 15 minutes | Cook time: 25 minutes

Ingredients:

- 1 whole chicken (about 3-4 lbs)
- 2 tablespoons extra-virgin olive oil
- 2 teaspoons sea salt
- 1 teaspoon freshly ground black pepper
- 1 tablespoon fresh rosemary, finely chopped
- 1 tablespoon fresh thyme, finely chopped
- 1 tablespoon fresh oregano, finely chopped
- 3 cloves garlic, minced
- 1 cup chicken broth
- 1 lemon, sliced

Directions:

1. In a bowl, combine olive oil, salt, black pepper, rosemary, thyme, oregano, and minced garlic to create a herb paste.
2. Rub the herb paste all over the chicken, both outside and under the skin where possible.
3. Place the trivet in the Instant Pot and add the chicken broth. Set the herb-coated chicken on the trivet.
4. Secure the Instant Pot lid, set the vent to "sealing", and cook on manual high pressure for 25 minutes. Once the cooking cycle is complete, let it naturally release for 15 minutes, then manually release any remaining pressure.
5. For a crispy skin, you can optionally broil the chicken in an oven for 5-7 minutes. Serve with lemon slices.

Nutritional Information: 470 calories, 40g protein, 5g carbohydrates, 30g fat, 1g fiber, 150mg cholesterol, 650mg sodium, 400mg potassium.

Mediterranean Pork Ribs

Yield: 4 servings | Prep time: 15 minutes | Cook time: 45 minutes

Ingredients:

- 2 lbs pork ribs
- 1/4 cup extra-virgin olive oil
- 1 tablespoon fresh rosemary, finely chopped
- 1 tablespoon fresh thyme, finely chopped
- 4 cloves garlic, minced
- 1 teaspoon sea salt
- 1/2 teaspoon freshly ground black pepper
- 1 cup chicken broth
- 1 lemon, zested and juiced
- 1/2 cup kalamata olives, pitted and chopped

Directions:

1. In a bowl, mix together olive oil, rosemary, thyme, garlic, salt, pepper, and lemon zest to create a marinade. Rub this mixture over the pork ribs, ensuring they are well coated. Let them marinate for at least 30 minutes.
2. Set the Instant Pot to 'Sauté' mode and brown the ribs briefly on all sides.
3. Pour in the chicken broth, lemon juice, and add the chopped olives. Secure the Instant Pot lid.
4. Cook on manual high pressure for 45 minutes. Once finished, allow a natural release for 15 minutes, then manually release any remaining pressure.

Nutritional Information: 590 calories, 38g protein, 6g carbohydrates, 45g fat, 2g fiber, 120mg cholesterol, 700mg sodium, 500mg potassium.

Chicken Kofta with Yogurt Sauce

Yield: 4 servings | Prep time: 20 minutes | Cook time: 15 minutes

Ingredients:

For the Chicken Kofta:
- 1 lb ground chicken
- 1/4 cup fresh parsley, finely chopped
- 1/4 cup fresh cilantro, finely chopped
- 1 small onion, finely chopped
- 2 cloves garlic, minced
- 1 teaspoon ground cumin
- 1 teaspoon ground coriander
- 1/2 teaspoon ground paprika
- 1/2 teaspoon sea salt
- 1/4 teaspoon black pepper
- 1 tablespoon olive oil (for sautéing)

For the Yogurt Sauce:
- 1 cup plain Greek yogurt
- 1 clove garlic, minced
- 1 tablespoon lemon juice
- 2 tablespoons fresh mint, finely chopped
- Salt and pepper to taste

Directions:

1. In a mixing bowl, combine ground chicken, parsley, cilantro, onion, garlic, cumin, coriander, paprika, salt, and pepper. Mix until well combined.
2. Shape the chicken mixture into small oval-shaped patties.
3. Set the Instant Pot to 'Sauté' mode and heat olive oil. Brown the koftas on both sides (around 2-3 minutes per side). Remove and set aside.
4. Add 1/2 cup of water to the pot, place the trivet inside, and arrange the koftas on top. Secure the lid and cook on manual high pressure for 10 minutes. Quick release after cooking.
5. While koftas are cooking, mix yogurt, garlic, lemon juice, mint, salt, and pepper in a bowl to make the sauce.
6. Serve koftas hot with the yogurt sauce.

Nutritional Information: 320 calories, 28g protein, 10g carbohydrates, 18g fat, 1g fiber, 100mg cholesterol, 450mg sodium, 600mg potassium.

Beef & Olive Stew
Yield: 4 servings | Prep time: 15 minutes | Cook time: 40 minutes

Ingredients:

- 1 lb beef stew meat, cubed
- 1 tablespoon olive oil
- 1 onion, finely chopped
- 2 cloves garlic, minced
- 1 red bell pepper, chopped
- 1 cup green olives, pitted and halved
- 1 can (14.5 oz) diced tomatoes
- 2 cups beef broth
- 1 teaspoon dried oregano
- 1/2 teaspoon ground cumin
- Salt and pepper to taste
- Fresh parsley for garnish

Directions:

1. Set the Instant Pot to 'Sauté' mode and heat the olive oil. Add the beef cubes and brown on all sides. Remove and set aside.
2. In the same pot, add onion, garlic, and red bell pepper. Sauté until soft, about 3-4 minutes.
3. Return the beef to the pot, add olives, diced tomatoes, beef broth, oregano, cumin, salt, and pepper. Mix well.
4. Close the lid and set the Instant Pot to 'Manual' or 'Pressure Cook' mode for 35 minutes. Allow natural release for 10 minutes, then quick release the remaining pressure.
5. Garnish with fresh parsley before serving.

Nutritional Information: 350 calories, 28g protein, 15g carbohydrates, 20g fat, 4g fiber, 70mg cholesterol, 800mg sodium, 650mg potassium.

Quick Chicken Souvlaki
Yield: 4 servings | Prep time: 10 minutes | Cook time: 12 minutes

Ingredients:

- 1.5 lbs boneless, skinless chicken breasts, cut into 1-inch cubes
- 3 tablespoons olive oil
- 4 cloves garlic, minced
- Juice of 1 lemon
- 1 teaspoon dried oregano
- Salt and pepper to taste
- 1/2 cup chicken broth
- Wooden or metal skewers (if wooden, pre-soaked for 30 minutes)
- Fresh parsley and lemon slices for garnish

Directions:

1. In a bowl, mix together olive oil, garlic, lemon juice, oregano, salt, and pepper. Add the chicken cubes and marinate for at least 10 minutes (longer for better flavor).
2. Thread the chicken cubes onto skewers, leaving a small space between each piece.
3. Add chicken broth to the Instant Pot. Place a trivet or steam rack inside and set the chicken skewers on top.
4. Close the lid and set the Instant Pot to 'Manual' or 'Pressure Cook' mode for 8 minutes. Allow a natural release for 4 minutes, then quick release the remaining pressure.
5. Garnish with fresh parsley and lemon slices before serving.

Nutritional Information: 260 calories, 35g protein, 3g carbohydrates, 12g fat, 0.5g fiber, 90mg cholesterol, 250mg sodium, 450mg potassium.

Braised Duck with Oranges & Olives

Yield: 4 servings | Prep time: 20 minutes | Cook time: 40 minutes

Ingredients:

- 2 duck breasts, skin on and scored
- 2 tablespoons olive oil
- 1 onion, thinly sliced
- 4 cloves garlic, minced
- 1 cup green olives, pitted
- Zest and juice of 2 oranges
- 1 cup chicken or duck broth
- 1 tablespoon fresh rosemary, chopped
- Salt and pepper to taste
- Fresh parsley and orange slices for garnish

Directions:

1. Set the Instant Pot to 'Sauté' mode. Once hot, add the olive oil. Season the duck breasts with salt and pepper and place them skin-side down in the pot. Cook until the skin is golden and crisp, about 6-8 minutes. Remove and set aside.
2. In the same pot, add the onions and garlic. Sauté until translucent. Add the olives, orange zest, juice, and rosemary, stirring well.
3. Return the duck breasts, skin-side up, to the pot. Add the broth. Close the lid and set the Instant Pot to 'Manual' or 'Pressure Cook' mode for 30 minutes.
4. Allow a natural release for 10 minutes, then quick release the remaining pressure. Garnish with fresh parsley and orange slices before serving.

Nutritional Information: 410 calories, 34g protein, 15g carbohydrates, 24g fat, 3g fiber, 85mg cholesterol, 750mg sodium, 580mg potassium.

Lamb & Chickpea Curry

Yield: 4 servings | Prep time: 15 minutes | Cook time: 35 minutes

Ingredients:

- 1 lb boneless lamb shoulder, cubed
- 2 tablespoons olive oil
- 1 large onion, finely chopped
- 3 garlic cloves, minced
- 1 tablespoon ginger, grated
- 1 can (15 oz) chickpeas, drained and rinsed
- 1 can (14 oz) diced tomatoes
- 2 teaspoons ground cumin
- 2 teaspoons ground coriander
- 1 teaspoon ground turmeric
- 1/2 teaspoon cayenne pepper (adjust to taste)
- 2 cups vegetable or chicken broth
- 1 tablespoon fresh lemon juice
- Salt and pepper to taste
- Fresh cilantro for garnish

Directions:

1. Set the Instant Pot to 'Sauté' mode. Add the olive oil. Once hot, brown the lamb cubes on all sides, working in batches to prevent overcrowding. Set aside.
2. In the same pot, add onions, garlic, and ginger. Sauté until the onions become translucent.
3. Stir in the chickpeas, tomatoes, cumin, coriander, turmeric, and cayenne pepper. Return the lamb cubes back to the pot.
4. Add broth, ensuring the meat and chickpeas are submerged. Close the lid, set the Instant Pot to 'Manual' or 'Pressure Cook' mode, and adjust to 30 minutes.
5. Once cooking is done, allow a natural release for 5 minutes, then quick release. Stir in lemon juice, adjust seasoning if necessary, and serve garnished with fresh cilantro.

Nutritional Information: 485 calories, 32g protein, 38g carbohydrates, 23g fat, 8g fiber, 85mg cholesterol, 570mg sodium, 670mg potassium.

Legumes & Lentils

Instant Pot Lentil Soup

Yield: 4 servings | Prep time: 10 minutes | Cook time: 25 minutes

Ingredients:

- 1 cup dried lentils (green or brown), rinsed and drained
- 1 tablespoon olive oil
- 1 medium onion, diced
- 2 carrots, chopped
- 2 celery stalks, chopped
- 3 garlic cloves, minced
- 1 teaspoon ground cumin
- 1/2 teaspoon ground turmeric
- 4 cups vegetable broth
- 1 can (14 oz) diced tomatoes
- 1 bay leaf
- Salt and pepper to taste
- 2 tablespoons fresh lemon juice
- Fresh parsley or cilantro for garnish

Directions:

1. Set the Instant Pot to 'Sauté' mode. Add olive oil, then sauté onions, carrots, and celery until softened. Add garlic and cook for another minute.
2. Add cumin, turmeric, lentils, broth, tomatoes, bay leaf, salt, and pepper. Stir to combine.
3. Secure the lid, set the Instant Pot to 'Manual' or 'Pressure Cook' mode, and adjust to 20 minutes.
4. Once cooking is complete, allow a natural release for 10 minutes, then quick release the remaining pressure. Remove the bay leaf, stir in lemon juice, adjust seasoning if necessary, and serve garnished with fresh parsley or cilantro.

Nutritional Information: 260 calories, 18g protein, 40g carbohydrates, 3.5g fat, 16g fiber, 0mg cholesterol, 580mg sodium, 740mg potassium.

Chickpea & Spinach Masala

Yield: 4 servings | Prep time: 15 minutes | Cook time: 20 minutes

Ingredients:

- 2 cups cooked chickpeas (or one 14 oz can, drained and rinsed)
- 1 tablespoon olive oil
- 1 medium onion, finely chopped
- 3 garlic cloves, minced
- 1-inch ginger, grated
- 1 can (14 oz) diced tomatoes
- 2 teaspoons garam masala
- 1 teaspoon ground cumin
- 1 teaspoon ground coriander
- 1/2 teaspoon turmeric
- 1/2 teaspoon red chili powder (adjust according to taste)
- Salt to taste
- 4 cups fresh spinach, roughly chopped
- 2 tablespoons fresh cilantro, chopped (optional, for garnish)
- Juice of half a lemon

Directions:

1. Set the Instant Pot to 'Sauté' mode. Add olive oil, followed by onions. Sauté until translucent. Add in garlic and ginger and sauté for an additional 1-2 minutes.
2. Add the diced tomatoes, garam masala, cumin, coriander, turmeric, chili powder, and salt. Mix well.
3. Add in chickpeas and stir, ensuring they are well coated with the masala.
4. Secure the lid, set the Instant Pot to 'Manual' or 'Pressure Cook' mode, and adjust to 10 minutes. After cooking, quick release the pressure.
5. Open the lid, stir in the fresh spinach, allowing it to wilt from the residual heat. Add lemon juice, adjust seasoning if necessary, and serve garnished with fresh cilantro.

Nutritional Information: 220 calories, 10g protein, 35g carbohydrates, 6g fat, 9g fiber, 0mg cholesterol, 320mg sodium, 620mg potassium.

Mediterranean Bean Stew

Yield: 4 servings | Prep time: 15 minutes | Cook time: 30 minutes

Ingredients:

- 1 tablespoon olive oil
- 1 medium onion, diced
- 3 garlic cloves, minced
- 1 bell pepper, diced
- 1 zucchini, diced
- 2 carrots, sliced
- 1 can (14 oz) white beans (e.g., cannellini or navy beans), drained and rinsed
- 1 can (14 oz) diced tomatoes with juice
- 3 cups vegetable broth
- 1 teaspoon dried oregano
- 1 teaspoon dried basil
- 1/2 teaspoon smoked paprika
- 1 bay leaf
- Salt and black pepper, to taste
- 1/4 cup fresh parsley, chopped
- Juice of half a lemon

Directions:

1. Turn on the Instant Pot's 'Sauté' mode. Add olive oil, onions, and garlic. Sauté until the onions are translucent.
2. Add the bell pepper, zucchini, and carrots. Continue sautéing for 2-3 minutes.
3. Add in the beans, diced tomatoes, vegetable broth, oregano, basil, smoked paprika, bay leaf, salt, and pepper. Stir well.
4. Close the Instant Pot lid and set it to 'Manual' or 'Pressure Cook' for 25 minutes. Once done, use the quick release method to release the pressure.
5. Open the lid, remove the bay leaf, and stir in the fresh parsley and lemon juice. Adjust seasoning if necessary before serving.

Nutritional Information: 240 calories, 11g protein, 45g carbohydrates, 3g fat, 12g fiber, 0mg cholesterol, 480mg sodium, 900mg potassium.

Lentils with Chorizo & Vegetables

Yield: 4 servings | Prep time: 20 minutes | Cook time: 25 minutes

Ingredients:

- 1 cup dried lentils, rinsed and drained
- 1 tablespoon olive oil
- 1 medium onion, diced
- 3 garlic cloves, minced
- 1 medium carrot, diced
- 1 bell pepper, diced
- 2 medium tomatoes, diced
- 3 ounces chorizo, sliced into rounds or chunks
- 2.5 cups vegetable broth or water
- 1 bay leaf
- 1 teaspoon smoked paprika
- Salt and black pepper, to taste
- 2 tablespoons fresh parsley, chopped
- Juice of half a lemon

Directions:

1. Turn on the Instant Pot's 'Sauté' mode. Add olive oil, chorizo, onions, and garlic. Sauté until the onions are translucent and chorizo releases its oils.
2. Add the carrot, bell pepper, and tomatoes, continuing to sauté for another 3-4 minutes.
3. Mix in the lentils, vegetable broth or water, bay leaf, smoked paprika, salt, and pepper. Ensure that the lentils are submerged.
4. Close the Instant Pot lid and set it to 'Manual' or 'Pressure Cook' for 20 minutes. Once done, use the quick release method to release the pressure.
5. Open the lid, remove the bay leaf, and stir in fresh parsley and lemon juice. Adjust seasoning if needed and serve warm.

Nutritional Information: 400 calories, 25g protein, 45g carbohydrates, 12g fat, 15g fiber, 25mg cholesterol, 650mg sodium, 700mg potassium.

Quick Falafel Mix

Yield: 4 servings | Prep time: 15 minutes | Cook time: 15 minutes

Ingredients:

- 2 cups dried chickpeas, soaked overnight and drained
- 1 medium onion, roughly chopped
- 3 garlic cloves
- 1 cup fresh parsley, packed
- 1 cup fresh cilantro, packed
- 1 teaspoon ground cumin
- 1 teaspoon ground coriander
- 1/2 teaspoon chili powder
- 1/2 teaspoon baking powder
- Salt to taste
- 2 tablespoons olive oil (for sautéing)

Directions:

1. In a food processor, combine the soaked chickpeas, onion, garlic, parsley, cilantro, cumin, coriander, chili powder, baking powder, and salt. Process until smooth but still a little grainy.
2. Turn on the Instant Pot's 'Sauté' mode. Add olive oil and let it heat.
3. Using your hands, form the chickpea mixture into small patties or balls. Place them in the Instant Pot and sauté until they're golden brown on both sides. You might need to work in batches.
4. Once cooked, transfer the falafels to a plate lined with paper towels to absorb any excess oil.

Nutritional Information: 320 calories, 15g protein, 50g carbohydrates, 7g fat, 13g fiber, 0mg cholesterol, 250mg sodium, 500mg potassium.

White Bean & Herb Soup

Yield: 4 servings | Prep time: 15 minutes | Cook time: 25 minutes

Ingredients:

- 2 cups dried white beans, soaked overnight
- 1 medium onion, finely chopped
- 3 cloves garlic, minced
- 4 cups vegetable broth
- 1 cup chopped tomatoes (canned or fresh)
- 2 teaspoons fresh thyme, minced
- 2 teaspoons fresh rosemary, minced
- 1 bay leaf
- 2 tablespoons olive oil
- Salt and pepper to taste
- Fresh parsley, for garnish
- Juice of half a lemon

Directions:

1. Turn the Instant Pot to 'Sauté' mode. Add the olive oil, onions, and garlic. Sauté until the onions are translucent.
2. Add the soaked white beans, vegetable broth, chopped tomatoes, thyme, rosemary, bay leaf, salt, and pepper. Stir well.
3. Close the lid, set the Instant Pot to 'High Pressure' for 25 minutes.
4. Once done, let the pressure release naturally. Remove the bay leaf. Add lemon juice and adjust the seasonings.
5. Serve hot, garnished with fresh parsley.

Nutritional Information: 380 calories, 20g protein, 62g carbohydrates, 6g fat, 15g fiber, 0mg cholesterol, 400mg sodium, 1,250mg potassium.

Black Eyed Peas in Tomato Sauce

Yield: 4 servings | Prep time: 10 minutes | Cook time: 30 minutes

Ingredients:

- 2 cups dried black-eyed peas, soaked for at least 4 hours or overnight
- 1 medium onion, diced
- 3 garlic cloves, minced
- 2 cups tomato sauce (canned or homemade)
- 3 cups vegetable broth or water
- 2 tablespoons olive oil
- 1 teaspoon smoked paprika
- 1 teaspoon ground cumin
- Salt and pepper to taste
- Fresh parsley or cilantro, for garnish
- 1 tablespoon lemon juice (optional)

Directions:

1. Set the Instant Pot to 'Sauté' mode. Add the olive oil, diced onions, and garlic. Sauté until the onions become translucent.
2. Add the drained black-eyed peas, tomato sauce, vegetable broth, smoked paprika, cumin, salt, and pepper. Stir to combine.
3. Close the Instant Pot lid, ensure the valve is set to 'Sealing', and cook on 'High Pressure' for 30 minutes.
4. Once the cooking is complete, allow for a natural pressure release. Adjust seasoning as needed and stir in lemon juice if desired.
5. Serve the peas in bowls, garnished with fresh parsley or cilantro.

Nutritional Information: 350 calories, 18g protein, 60g carbohydrates, 7g fat, 10g fiber, 0mg cholesterol, 580mg sodium, 1,100mg potassium.

Instant Pot Hummus

Yield: 4 servings | Prep time: 10 minutes | Cook time: 40 minutes

Ingredients:

- 1 cup dried chickpeas, soaked overnight and drained
- 3 cups water
- 3 garlic cloves
- 1/4 cup tahini
- 1/4 cup lemon juice
- 2 tablespoons olive oil
- 1 teaspoon ground cumin
- Salt to taste
- Paprika and extra olive oil for garnish

Directions:

1. In the Instant Pot, add soaked chickpeas and water. Close the lid and set the valve to 'Sealing'. Cook on 'High Pressure' for 40 minutes.
2. Once cooked, perform a quick pressure release. Drain the chickpeas, reserving about 1/2 cup of the cooking liquid.
3. In a blender or food processor, combine the cooked chickpeas, garlic, tahini, lemon juice, olive oil, cumin, and salt. Blend until smooth. If the mixture is too thick, add a bit of the reserved chickpea cooking liquid until desired consistency is reached.
4. Taste and adjust seasoning if necessary.
5. Transfer the hummus to a serving bowl, drizzle with additional olive oil, and sprinkle with paprika.

Nutritional Information: 270 calories, 8g protein, 30g carbohydrates, 14g fat, 7g fiber, 0mg cholesterol, 320mg sodium, 310mg potassium.

Chickpea & Saffron Soup

Yield: 4 servings | Prep time: 15 minutes | Cook time: 50 minutes

Ingredients:

- 1 cup dried chickpeas, soaked overnight and drained
- 1 large onion, diced
- 2 cloves garlic, minced
- 1 small pinch saffron threads
- 4 cups vegetable broth
- 2 tablespoons olive oil
- 1 teaspoon ground cumin
- 1 bay leaf
- Salt and pepper to taste
- Fresh parsley, chopped, for garnish

Directions:

1. Set the Instant Pot to 'Sauté' mode. Add olive oil, onions, and garlic. Cook until onions are translucent, about 3-5 minutes.
2. Add cumin and saffron threads, stirring for another 1 minute until fragrant.
3. Add the soaked chickpeas, vegetable broth, bay leaf, salt, and pepper. Close the lid and set the valve to 'Sealing'.
4. Cook on 'High Pressure' for 45 minutes. Once done, perform a quick pressure release.
5. Discard the bay leaf. Serve hot, garnished with fresh parsley.

Nutritional Information: 290 calories, 12g protein, 40g carbohydrates, 10g fat, 10g fiber, 0mg cholesterol, 480mg sodium, 380mg potassium.

Lentil & Vegetable Medley

Yield: 4 servings | Prep time: 15 minutes | Cook time: 25 minutes

Ingredients:

- 1 cup dried green lentils, rinsed and drained
- 2 medium carrots, diced
- 1 zucchini, diced
- 1 bell pepper, diced
- 1 onion, diced
- 2 cloves garlic, minced
- 1 can (14 oz) diced tomatoes
- 4 cups vegetable broth
- 2 tablespoons olive oil
- 1 teaspoon dried oregano
- 1/2 teaspoon smoked paprika
- Salt and pepper to taste
- Fresh basil or parsley, chopped, for garnish

Directions:

1. Turn on the Instant Pot to 'Sauté' mode. Add olive oil followed by onions and garlic. Cook until onions are translucent, about 3-5 minutes.
2. Add the carrots, zucchini, bell pepper, oregano, smoked paprika, salt, and pepper. Stir and sauté for another 2-3 minutes.
3. Add the lentils, diced tomatoes, and vegetable broth. Stir well.
4. Secure the lid and set the valve to 'Sealing'. Cook on 'High Pressure' for 20 minutes. After the cooking cycle is complete, allow a natural pressure release for 5 minutes, then perform a quick release.
5. Adjust seasonings if needed and serve hot, garnished with fresh basil or parsley.

Nutritional Information: 290 calories, 15g protein, 45g carbohydrates, 7g fat, 15g fiber, 0mg cholesterol, 550mg sodium, 780mg potassium.

Pasta & Risottos

Instant Seafood Linguine

Yield: 4 servings | Prep time: 20 minutes | Cook time: 8 minutes

Ingredients:

- 8 oz linguine
- 1 lb mixed seafood (shrimp, mussels, squid, scallops)
- 2 tablespoons olive oil
- 1 onion, finely chopped
- 3 garlic cloves, minced
- 1 can (14 oz) crushed tomatoes
- 1/4 cup white wine
- 1/4 cup fresh parsley, chopped
- 1/2 teaspoon chili flakes (optional)
- Salt and pepper to taste
- Zest and juice of 1 lemon
- 2 cups water or seafood stock

Directions:

1. Turn on the Instant Pot to 'Sauté' mode. Add olive oil followed by onions and garlic. Sauté until the onions are translucent, about 2-3 minutes.
2. Add the crushed tomatoes, white wine, chili flakes, lemon zest, salt, and pepper. Stir well.
3. Break the linguine in half and spread it over the sauce in the pot. Pour in the water or seafood stock, ensuring the linguine is submerged.
4. Secure the lid and set the valve to 'Sealing'. Cook on 'High Pressure' for 4 minutes. Once done, perform a quick release. Open the lid and stir in the mixed seafood. Close the lid and let it sit for another 3-4 minutes, allowing the seafood to cook in the residual heat.
5. Stir in lemon juice and adjust seasonings if necessary. Serve hot, garnished with fresh parsley.

Nutritional Information: 420 calories, 28g protein, 52g carbohydrates, 10g fat, 4g fiber, 130mg cholesterol, 580mg sodium, 580mg potassium.

Mushroom & Truffle Risotto

Yield: 4 servings | Prep time: 15 minutes | Cook time: 7 minutes

Ingredients:

- 1 cup Arborio rice
- 2 cups mushrooms, sliced (such as cremini, shiitake, or oyster)
- 1 small onion, finely chopped
- 2 cloves garlic, minced
- 2 tablespoons olive oil
- 1/4 cup white wine
- 2.5 cups vegetable broth
- 2 tablespoons truffle oil
- 1/4 cup Parmesan cheese, grated
- Salt and black pepper to taste
- 1/4 cup fresh parsley, chopped

Directions:

1. Set the Instant Pot to 'Sauté' mode. Add the olive oil, followed by onions and garlic. Sauté until the onions become translucent, about 2-3 minutes. Add the mushrooms and continue to sauté until softened.
2. Add the Arborio rice to the pot and stir, letting it toast slightly for about a minute. Pour in the white wine and let it evaporate, another 1-2 minutes.
3. Add the vegetable broth, salt, and pepper, stirring well. Secure the Instant Pot lid and set the valve to 'Sealing'. Cook on 'High Pressure' for 5 minutes. Once done, perform a quick release.
4. Stir in the truffle oil and Parmesan cheese until creamy and well combined. Adjust seasoning if necessary. Serve hot and garnish with freshly chopped parsley.

Nutritional Information: 380 calories, 8g protein, 51g carbohydrates, 14g fat, 2g fiber, 10mg cholesterol, 590mg sodium, 300mg potassium.

Pasta Puttanesca in a Flash

Yield: 4 servings | Prep time: 10 minutes | Cook time: 8 minutes

Ingredients:

- 8 oz spaghetti or linguine
- 1 can (14 oz) diced tomatoes with juice
- 3 cloves garlic, minced
- 2 tablespoons olive oil
- 2 tablespoons capers, drained
- 1/4 cup pitted black olives, sliced
- 1 teaspoon anchovy paste (optional)
- 1/4 teaspoon red pepper flakes
- 1/4 cup fresh parsley, chopped
- 1/4 cup fresh basil, chopped
- Salt to taste
- 2 cups water

Directions:

1. Set the Instant Pot to 'Sauté' mode. Add olive oil, garlic, anchovy paste (if using), and red pepper flakes. Sauté for about 1 minute until fragrant.
2. Add in the diced tomatoes, capers, and olives. Stir to combine.
3. Break the pasta in half and add to the pot. Pour water over the pasta, ensuring that it's submerged. Season with salt.
4. Secure the Instant Pot lid and set the valve to 'Sealing'. Cook on 'High Pressure' for 4 minutes. Once done, perform a quick release.
5. Stir in fresh parsley and basil, combining well. Serve hot and adjust seasoning if needed.

Nutritional Information: 330 calories, 9g protein, 49g carbohydrates, 11g fat, 3g fiber, 5mg cholesterol, 650mg sodium, 360mg potassium.

Pressure-Cooked Orzo & Shrimp

Yield: 4 servings | Prep time: 15 minutes | Cook time: 7 minutes

Ingredients:

- 1 cup orzo pasta
- 1 pound large shrimp, peeled and deveined
- 2 tablespoons olive oil
- 3 cloves garlic, minced
- 1 medium onion, finely chopped
- 1 can (14 oz) diced tomatoes with juice
- 2 cups vegetable broth or water
- 1/4 cup fresh parsley, chopped
- 1/4 teaspoon red pepper flakes (optional)
- Zest and juice of 1 lemon
- Salt and pepper to taste

Directions:

1. Set the Instant Pot to 'Sauté' mode. Add olive oil, garlic, and onion. Sauté until the onion becomes translucent, about 3 minutes.
2. Add orzo, diced tomatoes, lemon zest, red pepper flakes, and vegetable broth to the pot. Mix well.
3. Secure the Instant Pot lid and set the valve to 'Sealing'. Cook on 'High Pressure' for 3 minutes.
4. Perform a quick release, then add in the shrimp, stirring well. Place the lid back on (without sealing) and let the residual heat cook the shrimp for about 3-4 minutes, or until pink.
5. Stir in fresh parsley, lemon juice, and adjust seasoning with salt and pepper. Serve immediately.

Nutritional Information: 360 calories, 29g protein, 45g carbohydrates, 7g fat, 2g fiber, 165mg cholesterol, 580mg sodium, 320mg potassium.

Tomato & Basil Penne

Yield: 4 servings | Prep time: 10 minutes | Cook time: 8 minutes

Ingredients:

- 2 cups penne pasta
- 1 can (28 oz) whole peeled tomatoes
- 3 cloves garlic, minced
- 1/4 cup fresh basil, chopped
- 2 tablespoons olive oil
- 1/4 cup grated Parmesan cheese
- 1/2 teaspoon red pepper flakes (optional)
- Salt and pepper to taste
- 2 cups water

Directions:

1. Set the Instant Pot to 'Sauté' mode. Add olive oil and garlic. Sauté until the garlic becomes fragrant, about 1-2 minutes.
2. Add whole peeled tomatoes, breaking them up with a spoon, followed by the penne, water, salt, and pepper. Mix well to ensure that the pasta is submerged in the liquid.
3. Secure the Instant Pot lid, set the valve to 'Sealing'. Cook on 'High Pressure' for 6 minutes.
4. Perform a quick release, then stir in the fresh basil, red pepper flakes, and grated Parmesan cheese. Adjust seasoning as needed and serve.

Nutritional Information: 320 calories, 12g protein, 52g carbohydrates, 8g fat, 3g fiber, 10mg cholesterol, 320mg sodium, 400mg potassium.

Creamy Spinach Risotto

Yield: 4 servings | Prep time: 10 minutes | Cook time: 20 minutes

Ingredients:

- 1 cup Arborio rice
- 2 tablespoons olive oil
- 1 small onion, finely chopped
- 2 cloves garlic, minced
- 1/4 cup white wine (optional)
- 3 cups vegetable broth
- 2 cups fresh spinach, roughly chopped
- 1/2 cup grated Parmesan cheese
- 1/4 cup heavy cream
- Salt and pepper to taste
- 1 tablespoon lemon zest (optional)

Directions:

1. Set the Instant Pot to 'Sauté' mode. Add olive oil, chopped onion, and garlic. Sauté until onions are translucent, about 3-4 minutes.
2. Add Arborio rice to the pot and stir for about 2 minutes until the grains are well-coated in the oil. Pour in the white wine (if using) and let it simmer until mostly evaporated.
3. Add the vegetable broth, making sure the rice is fully submerged. Secure the lid, set the valve to 'Sealing', and set the Instant Pot to 'High Pressure' for 6 minutes.
4. Once done, perform a quick release. Stir in the chopped spinach, allowing the residual heat to wilt the spinach. Finally, mix in the heavy cream and Parmesan cheese. Adjust seasoning with salt, pepper, and lemon zest (if desired). Serve immediately.

Nutritional Information: 400 calories, 12g protein, 55g carbohydrates, 14g fat, 2g fiber, 35mg cholesterol, 500mg sodium, 200mg potassium.

Mediterranean Mac 'n' Cheese

Yield: 4 servings | Prep time: 15 minutes | Cook time: 12 minutes

Ingredients:

- 8 oz. whole wheat macaroni
- 2 tablespoons olive oil
- 1/4 cup sun-dried tomatoes, chopped
- 1/4 cup Kalamata olives, pitted and chopped
- 1/4 cup feta cheese, crumbled
- 1 cup mozzarella cheese, shredded
- 2 cloves garlic, minced
- 2 1/2 cups vegetable broth
- 1/2 cup heavy cream
- 2 cups fresh spinach
- 1 teaspoon dried oregano
- Salt and pepper to taste
- Fresh basil or parsley for garnish (optional)

Directions:

1. Set the Instant Pot to 'Sauté' mode. Add olive oil and garlic, sautéing for 2 minutes. Then, add in sun-dried tomatoes and olives, cooking for another 2 minutes.
2. Pour in the vegetable broth followed by the macaroni. Stir well to ensure the pasta is submerged in the broth.
3. Secure the lid, set the valve to 'Sealing', and set the Instant Pot to 'High Pressure' for 5 minutes. Once done, perform a quick release.
4. Stir in heavy cream, feta cheese, mozzarella cheese, and oregano. Continue stirring until cheeses melt into a creamy sauce. Fold in fresh spinach until it wilts. Season with salt and pepper to taste. Garnish with fresh herbs, if desired, before serving.

Nutritional Information: 500 calories, 20g protein, 60g carbohydrates, 23g fat, 8g fiber, 70mg cholesterol, 750mg sodium, 320mg potassium.

Spaghetti with Instant Meatballs

Yield: 4 servings | Prep time: 20 minutes | Cook time: 15 minutes

Ingredients:

- 8 oz. whole wheat spaghetti
- 1 lb. lean ground turkey or beef
- 1/4 cup whole wheat bread crumbs
- 2 cloves garlic, minced
- 1/4 cup grated Parmesan cheese
- 1 large egg
- 1 teaspoon dried oregano
- 1 teaspoon dried basil
- 1/2 teaspoon salt
- 1/4 teaspoon black pepper
- 2 cups marinara sauce (store-bought or homemade)
- 2 tablespoons fresh parsley, chopped
- 2 tablespoons olive oil
- 1 cup water or broth

Directions:

1. In a large mixing bowl, combine ground meat, bread crumbs, garlic, Parmesan cheese, egg, oregano, basil, salt, and pepper. Mix until well combined, then form into small meatballs, roughly the size of a golf ball.
2. Set the Instant Pot to 'Sauté' mode. Add olive oil and brown the meatballs on all sides, about 3-4 minutes. Remove meatballs and set aside.
3. Add water or broth to the Instant Pot, making sure to scrape up any brown bits from the bottom. Break spaghetti in half and place them in the pot, spreading them out to prevent clumping. Pour marinara sauce over the spaghetti, ensuring the pasta is covered. Place meatballs on top.
4. Secure the lid, set the valve to 'Sealing', and set the Instant Pot to 'High Pressure' for 8 minutes. Once done, perform a quick release. Stir gently, garnish with fresh parsley, and serve immediately.

Nutritional Information: 550 calories, 30g protein, 65g carbohydrates, 20g fat, 7g fiber, 100mg cholesterol, 600mg sodium, 650mg potassium.

Sausage & Pepper Pasta

Yield: 4 servings | Prep time: 15 minutes | Cook time: 10 minutes

Ingredients:

- 8 oz. whole wheat penne pasta
- 1 lb. chicken or turkey sausage, sliced into rounds
- 1 tablespoon olive oil
- 1 large red bell pepper, sliced
- 1 large yellow bell pepper, sliced
- 1 large onion, sliced
- 3 cloves garlic, minced
- 2 cups crushed tomatoes (no added sugar)
- 1 teaspoon dried oregano
- 1 teaspoon dried basil
- Salt and pepper to taste
- 1/4 cup fresh parsley, chopped (for garnish)
- 1 cup water

Directions:

1. Set the Instant Pot to 'Sauté' mode. Add olive oil, sliced sausage, bell peppers, and onion. Sauté for 5 minutes until the vegetables are slightly tender and the sausage is browned.
2. Add garlic, crushed tomatoes, oregano, basil, salt, and pepper. Stir to combine.
3. Add the pasta to the pot, followed by water, ensuring the pasta is submerged under the liquid.
4. Secure the lid, set the valve to 'Sealing', and set the Instant Pot to 'High Pressure' for 5 minutes. Once done, perform a quick release. Stir gently to combine, taste for seasoning adjustments, garnish with fresh parsley, and serve immediately.

Nutritional Information: 480 calories, 28g protein, 65g carbohydrates, 13g fat, 8g fiber, 70mg cholesterol, 580mg sodium, 670mg potassium.

Lemon & Asparagus Risotto

Yield: 4 servings | Prep time: 10 minutes | Cook time: 20 minutes

Ingredients:

- 1 cup Arborio rice
- 2 tablespoons olive oil
- 1 small onion, finely chopped
- 3 cloves garlic, minced
- 3 cups vegetable broth
- Zest and juice of 1 lemon
- 1 bunch asparagus, woody ends removed and chopped into 1-inch pieces
- 1/2 cup freshly grated Parmesan cheese (optional for dairy-free or vegan diets)
- Salt and pepper to taste
- Fresh parsley or basil for garnish

Directions:

1. Set the Instant Pot to 'Sauté' mode. Add olive oil, onion, and garlic. Sauté until the onions are translucent.
2. Add Arborio rice to the pot and stir for 2 minutes to lightly toast the rice.
3. Pour in vegetable broth, lemon zest, and juice. Give it a quick stir to combine.
4. Secure the lid, set the valve to 'Sealing', and set the Instant Pot to 'High Pressure' for 6 minutes. After cooking, allow the pressure to naturally release for 10 minutes, then perform a quick release.
5. Stir in the chopped asparagus, allowing the residual heat to cook it slightly. Mix in Parmesan cheese until melted and creamy. Season with salt and pepper to taste, and garnish with fresh herbs before serving.

Nutritional Information: 340 calories, 9g protein, 53g carbohydrates, 11g fat, 3g fiber, 10mg cholesterol, 620mg sodium, 300mg potassium.

Soups & Stews

Minestrone in Minutes

Yield: 4 servings | Prep time: 15 minutes | Cook time: 8 minutes

Ingredients:

- 2 tablespoons olive oil
- 1 onion, diced
- 3 cloves garlic, minced
- 1 carrot, diced
- 1 celery stalk, diced
- 1 zucchini, diced
- 1 cup green beans, chopped
- 1 can (14.5 oz) diced tomatoes
- 4 cups vegetable broth
- 1/2 cup elbow pasta or small shell pasta
- 1 can (15 oz) cannellini beans, rinsed and drained
- 1 teaspoon dried oregano
- 1 teaspoon dried basil
- Salt and pepper to taste
- 2 cups baby spinach
- Grated Parmesan cheese for garnish (optional)

Directions:

1. Set the Instant Pot to 'Sauté' mode. Add olive oil, followed by onion, garlic, carrot, and celery. Sauté until onions are translucent.
2. Add zucchini, green beans, tomatoes, vegetable broth, pasta, beans, oregano, basil, salt, and pepper. Stir to combine.
3. Secure the lid, set the valve to 'Sealing', and set the Instant Pot to 'High Pressure' for 4 minutes.
4. Once done, quickly release the pressure. Open the lid, stir in baby spinach until wilted. Adjust seasoning if necessary. Serve hot, garnished with grated Parmesan cheese if desired y.

Nutritional Information: 280 calories, 11g protein, 45g carbohydrates, 7g fat, 10g fiber, 0mg cholesterol, 780mg sodium, 850mg potassium.

Instant Pot Bouillabaisse

Yield: 4 servings | Prep time: 20 minutes | Cook time: 15 minutes

Ingredients:

- 2 tablespoons olive oil
- 1 onion, finely chopped
- 3 cloves garlic, minced
- 1 fennel bulb, thinly sliced
- 1 can (14.5 oz) diced tomatoes
- 4 cups fish stock or seafood broth
- 1 cup white wine
- 1 teaspoon saffron threads
- 1 bay leaf
- 1 teaspoon dried thyme
- 1/2 teaspoon orange zest
- 1/2 pound firm white fish (like cod), cut into chunks
- 1/2 pound mussels, cleaned
- 1/2 pound large shrimp, peeled and deveined
- 1/4 cup fresh parsley, chopped
- Salt and pepper to taste
- 1 baguette, sliced and toasted, for serving

Directions:

1. Set the Instant Pot to 'Sauté' mode. Add olive oil, followed by onion, garlic, and fennel. Sauté until softened, around 5 minutes.
2. Add the diced tomatoes, fish stock, white wine, saffron, bay leaf, thyme, and orange zest to the pot. Stir to combine.
3. Add in the fish chunks, mussels, and shrimp. Secure the lid, set the valve to 'Sealing', and set the Instant Pot to 'High Pressure' for 5 minutes.
4. Once done, carefully release the pressure. Remove the bay leaf and adjust seasoning with salt and pepper. Stir in fresh parsley.
5. Serve the bouillabaisse hot with toasted baguette slices.

Nutritional Information: 320 calories, 28g protein, 20g carbohydrates, 9g fat, 3g fiber, 95mg cholesterol, 700mg sodium, 600mg potassium.

The Quick Version

Eggplant & Lentil Soup

Yield: 4 servings | Prep time: 15 minutes | Cook time: 20 minutes

Ingredients:

- 2 tablespoons olive oil
- 1 medium onion, chopped
- 3 cloves garlic, minced
- 1 large eggplant, diced
- 1 cup dried lentils, rinsed and drained (preferably green or brown)
- 1 can (14.5 oz) diced tomatoes
- 4 cups vegetable broth
- 1 teaspoon ground cumin
- 1/2 teaspoon smoked paprika
- 1/2 teaspoon dried thyme
- Salt and pepper to taste
- 2 tablespoons fresh lemon juice
- 1/4 cup fresh parsley, chopped (for garnish)

Directions:

1. Set the Instant Pot to 'Sauté' mode. Add olive oil, followed by onion and garlic. Sauté until translucent, about 3 minutes.
2. Add the diced eggplant and cook for another 5 minutes, until it starts to soften.
3. Stir in the lentils, diced tomatoes, vegetable broth, cumin, smoked paprika, thyme, salt, and pepper. Mix well.
4. Close the lid, set the valve to 'Sealing', and cook on 'High Pressure' for 15 minutes.
5. Once done, carefully release the pressure. Stir in the fresh lemon juice. Adjust seasoning if needed and serve garnished with chopped parsley.

Nutritional Information: 310 calories, 18g protein, 46g carbohydrates, 7g fat, 20g fiber, 0mg cholesterol, 650mg sodium, 800mg potassium.

Chilled Cucumber & Yogurt Soup

Yield: 4 servings | Prep time: 15 minutes | Cook time: 5 minutes (plus cooling time)

Ingredients:

- 3 large cucumbers, peeled, seeded and chopped
- 2 cups Greek yogurt
- 2 cloves garlic, minced
- 2 tablespoons fresh dill, chopped
- 2 tablespoons fresh mint, chopped
- 1 tablespoon olive oil
- Juice of 1 lemon
- Salt and pepper to taste
- 1 cup water or vegetable broth
- Fresh dill sprigs for garnish

Directions:

1. Set the Instant Pot to 'Sauté' mode. Add olive oil and minced garlic, and sauté for about 2 minutes until fragrant. Turn off the pot.
2. Add chopped cucumbers, yogurt, dill, mint, lemon juice, and water or vegetable broth to the pot. Mix well.
3. Using an immersion blender, puree the mixture until smooth. Alternatively, you can blend the soup in batches using a regular blender.
4. Season with salt and pepper to taste. Chill the soup in the refrigerator for at least 2 hours before serving.
5. Serve cold, garnished with fresh dill sprigs.

Nutritional Information: 150 calories, 8g protein, 12g carbohydrates, 8g fat, 2g fiber, 10mg cholesterol, 80mg sodium, 400mg potassium.

Instant Pot Fisherman's Stew

Yield: 4 servings | Prep time: 20 minutes | Cook time: 15 minutes

Ingredients:

- 1 lb white fish fillets (such as cod or halibut), cut into chunks
- 12 large shrimp, peeled and deveined
- 1 cup mussels, cleaned and debearded
- 2 tablespoons olive oil
- 1 onion, diced
- 3 garlic cloves, minced
- 1 red bell pepper, sliced
- 1 cup cherry tomatoes, halved
- 2 cups fish stock or broth
- 1/2 cup white wine (optional)
- 1 teaspoon paprika
- 1 bay leaf
- 1/4 cup fresh parsley, chopped
- Salt and pepper to taste
- 1 lemon, juiced and zest

Directions:

1. Set the Instant Pot to 'Sauté' mode. Add olive oil, onions, garlic, and bell pepper. Sauté until the onions are translucent, about 3 minutes.
2. Add the white wine (if using), fish stock, cherry tomatoes, paprika, bay leaf, salt, and pepper. Stir well.
3. Place the fish chunks, shrimp, and mussels on top of the vegetable mixture.
4. Secure the Instant Pot lid and set to 'High Pressure' for 5 minutes. Once done, use the quick release method to release the pressure.
5. Stir in the lemon juice, lemon zest, and fresh parsley before serving. Adjust salt and pepper as needed.

Nutritional Information: 320 calories, 35g protein, 14g carbohydrates, 12g fat, 2g fiber, 90mg cholesterol, 480mg sodium, 620mg potassium.

Chickpea & Spinach Soup

Yield: 4 servings | Prep time: 15 minutes | Cook time: 20 minutes

Ingredients:

- 2 cups dried chickpeas, soaked overnight and drained
- 6 cups vegetable broth or water
- 2 tablespoons olive oil
- 1 onion, diced
- 3 garlic cloves, minced
- 1 teaspoon ground cumin
- 1/2 teaspoon ground turmeric
- 1/4 teaspoon cayenne pepper (optional)
- 2 cups fresh spinach, chopped
- Salt and pepper to taste
- 2 tablespoons fresh lemon juice
- 1/4 cup fresh cilantro, chopped (optional for garnish)

Directions:

1. Set the Instant Pot to 'Sauté' mode. Add olive oil, onions, and garlic. Sauté until the onions are translucent, about 3 minutes.
2. Add cumin, turmeric, and cayenne pepper, stirring for another minute until aromatic.
3. Add the soaked chickpeas and vegetable broth. Secure the Instant Pot lid and set to 'High Pressure' for 15 minutes.
4. Once done, use the quick release method to release the pressure. Stir in the fresh spinach, allowing it to wilt in the hot soup. Add the lemon juice and season with salt and pepper as needed.
5. Serve hot, garnished with fresh cilantro if desired.

Nutritional Information: 310 calories, 15g protein, 45g carbohydrates, 9g fat, 12g fiber, 0mg cholesterol, 480mg sodium, 720mg potassium.

Lamb & Vegetable Stew

Yield: 4 servings | Prep time: 20 minutes | Cook time: 40 minutes

Ingredients:

- 1 lb boneless lamb chunks, fat trimmed
- 2 tablespoons olive oil
- 1 onion, chopped
- 3 garlic cloves, minced
- 2 carrots, sliced into rounds
- 2 potatoes, diced
- 1 zucchini, diced
- 2 cups diced tomatoes (canned or fresh)
- 4 cups beef or vegetable broth
- 1 teaspoon dried rosemary
- 1 teaspoon dried thyme
- Salt and pepper to taste
- Fresh parsley, chopped (for garnish)

Directions:

1. Set the Instant Pot to 'Sauté' mode. Add olive oil, onions, and garlic. Sauté until the onions are translucent, about 3 minutes.
2. Add lamb chunks and brown on all sides, approximately 5 minutes.
3. Add carrots, potatoes, zucchini, tomatoes, broth, rosemary, thyme, salt, and pepper. Stir well.
4. Close the Instant Pot lid and set to 'Meat/Stew' mode or 'High Pressure' for 35 minutes. After cooking, allow pressure to release naturally for about 10 minutes, then quick release.
5. Serve hot and garnish with fresh parsley.

Nutritional Information: 410 calories, 28g protein, 35g carbohydrates, 18g fat, 6g fiber, 75mg cholesterol, 600mg sodium, 1200mg potassium.

Mediterranean Broth with Pasta & Beans

Yield: 4 servings | Prep time: 15 minutes | Cook time: 30 minutes

Ingredients:

- 1 cup pasta (whole wheat or regular)
- 2 tablespoons olive oil
- 1 onion, finely chopped
- 3 cloves garlic, minced
- 1 can (15 oz) white beans (like cannellini), rinsed and drained
- 1 can (15 oz) diced tomatoes, with juice
- 5 cups vegetable broth
- 1 cup chopped spinach or kale
- 2 teaspoons dried basil
- 1 teaspoon dried oregano
- Salt and pepper to taste
- Grated Parmesan cheese and fresh basil leaves (for garnish, optional)

Directions:

1. Set the Instant Pot to 'Sauté' mode. Add olive oil, onions, and garlic. Sauté until the onions are translucent, about 3-4 minutes.
2. Add beans, diced tomatoes, vegetable broth, dried basil, oregano, salt, and pepper. Stir to combine.
3. Add the pasta and mix well. Make sure the pasta is submerged in the broth.
4. Secure the Instant Pot lid and set to 'Manual' or 'High Pressure' mode for 6 minutes. Once done, allow pressure to release naturally for 5 minutes, then perform a quick release.
5. Stir in the chopped spinach or kale until wilted. Adjust seasoning if necessary. Serve hot, garnished with grated Parmesan cheese and fresh basil leaves.

Nutritional Information: 320 calories, 14g protein, 55g carbohydrates, 7g fat, 10g fiber, 5mg cholesterol, 800mg sodium, 900mg potassium.

Spicy Tomato & Chorizo Soup

Yield: 4 servings | Prep time: 10 minutes | Cook time: 20 minutes

Ingredients:

- 1 tablespoon olive oil
- 1 onion, diced
- 3 cloves garlic, minced
- 200 grams (7 oz) chorizo, sliced into rounds (opt for leaner variants for healthier option)
- 2 cans (15 oz each) diced tomatoes with their juice
- 3 cups chicken or vegetable broth
- 1 teaspoon smoked paprika
- 1/2 teaspoon chili flakes (adjust to taste)
- Salt and pepper to taste
- Fresh parsley, chopped (for garnish)

Directions:

1. Set the Instant Pot to 'Sauté' mode. Add olive oil, onion, garlic, and chorizo. Cook until onion is translucent and chorizo is lightly browned, about 4-5 minutes.
2. Add the diced tomatoes with their juice, broth, smoked paprika, chili flakes, salt, and pepper. Stir everything together to combine.
3. Secure the Instant Pot lid and set to 'Manual' or 'High Pressure' mode for 10 minutes. Once done, allow pressure to release naturally for 5 minutes, then perform a quick release.
4. Before serving, check for seasoning and adjust if necessary. Ladle into bowls and garnish with fresh parsley.

Nutritional Information: 320 calories, 15g protein, 25g carbohydrates, 20g fat, 5g fiber, 40mg cholesterol, 1,200mg sodium, 650mg potassium.

Sauces & Dips

Quick Tzatziki

Yield: 4 servings | Prep time: 10 minutes | Cook time: 0 minutes (as it's a cold dish)

Ingredients:

- 2 cups Greek yogurt (full-fat for traditional, but can use low-fat for a lighter version)
- 1 medium cucumber, finely grated and excess water squeezed out
- 3 cloves garlic, finely minced
- 1 tablespoon fresh dill, chopped
- 1 tablespoon lemon juice
- 1 tablespoon olive oil
- Salt and pepper to taste

Directions:

1. In a bowl, combine Greek yogurt, grated cucumber, and minced garlic.
2. Add in fresh dill, lemon juice, and olive oil. Stir well until all ingredients are well mixed.
3. Season with salt and pepper according to taste.
4. Chill in the refrigerator for at least 30 minutes before serving to allow flavors to meld.

Nutritional Information: 120 calories, 8g protein, 6g carbohydrates, 7g fat, 0.5g fiber, 5mg cholesterol, 60mg sodium, 200mg potassium.

Instant Pot Romesco Sauce

Yield: 4 servings | Prep time: 10 minutes | Cook time: 20 minutes

Ingredients:

- 1 large red bell pepper, seeded and cut into large chunks
- 1 large tomato, quartered
- 3 garlic cloves, peeled
- 1/2 cup raw almonds
- 1/4 cup hazelnuts
- 2 tablespoons olive oil
- 1 tablespoon sherry or red wine vinegar
- 1 teaspoon smoked paprika
- 1/4 teaspoon red chili flakes (optional for extra heat)
- Salt and pepper to taste

Directions:

1. Place red bell pepper, tomato, and garlic into the Instant Pot. Secure the lid.
2. Set the Instant Pot to manual pressure on high for 10 minutes. Once done, quick release the pressure.
3. Drain any excess liquid. Add almonds, hazelnuts, olive oil, vinegar, smoked paprika, and chili flakes (if using) to the Instant Pot contents.
4. Using an immersion blender or transferring to a regular blender, purée the mixture until smooth. Season with salt and pepper to taste.

Nutritional Information: 210 calories, 5g protein, 10g carbohydrates, 18g fat, 3g fiber, 0mg cholesterol, 8mg sodium, 320mg potassium.

Garlic & Herb Olive Spread

Yield: 4 servings | Prep time: 10 minutes | Cook time: 5 minutes

Ingredients:

- 1 cup green olives, pitted
- 1 cup black olives, pitted
- 4 garlic cloves
- 1/4 cup fresh parsley, chopped
- 1/4 cup fresh basil, chopped
- 2 tablespoons fresh lemon juice
- 1/4 cup extra virgin olive oil
- Salt and pepper to taste

Directions:

1. Place garlic cloves in the Instant Pot and add a cup of water. Secure the lid.
2. Set the Instant Pot to manual pressure on high for 5 minutes. Once done, quick release the pressure.
3. Remove garlic and discard the water. In the Instant Pot, combine steamed garlic, green and black olives, parsley, basil, lemon juice, and olive oil.
4. Using an immersion blender, blend the mixture until it reaches a spread-like consistency. Season with salt and pepper to taste.

Nutritional Information: 190 calories, 1g protein, 5g carbohydrates, 18g fat, 3g fiber, 0mg cholesterol, 650mg sodium, 50mg potassium.

Pressure-Cooked Marinara

Yield: 4 servings | Prep time: 15 minutes | Cook time: 20 minutes

Ingredients:

- 1 tablespoon extra virgin olive oil
- 1 medium onion, finely chopped
- 4 garlic cloves, minced
- 1 can (28 oz) crushed tomatoes
- 1/4 cup fresh basil, chopped
- 2 teaspoons fresh oregano, chopped (or 1 teaspoon dried)
- 1 bay leaf
- 1/2 teaspoon sugar (optional)
- Salt and pepper to taste

Directions:

1. Set Instant Pot to sauté mode and add olive oil. Once hot, add onions and sauté until translucent, about 3 minutes. Add garlic and sauté for an additional minute.
2. Stir in crushed tomatoes, basil, oregano, bay leaf, and sugar. Season with salt and pepper.
3. Secure the Instant Pot lid, set to manual pressure on high for 20 minutes.
4. Once cooking is complete, allow for a natural release for 10 minutes, then perform a quick release. Remove bay leaf before serving.

Nutritional Information: 90 calories, 2g protein, 13g carbohydrates, 4g fat, 3g fiber, 0mg cholesterol, 420mg sodium, 450mg potassium.

Tapenade in a Flash

Yield: 4 servings | Prep time: 10 minutes | Cook time: 0 minutes (Instant Pot not required for cooking)

Ingredients:

- 1 cup pitted Kalamata olives
- 2 garlic cloves
- 1 tablespoon capers, rinsed and drained
- 2 anchovy fillets (optional for a more authentic taste)
- 1 teaspoon fresh lemon juice
- 1 teaspoon lemon zest
- 2 tablespoons extra virgin olive oil
- Freshly ground black pepper to taste

Directions:

1. Place olives, garlic, capers, anchovies (if using), lemon juice, and lemon zest in a food processor.
2. Pulse several times to coarsely chop the ingredients.
3. With the food processor running, slowly drizzle in the olive oil until the tapenade reaches your desired consistency.
4. Taste and adjust seasoning with freshly ground black pepper. Transfer to a serving dish.

Nutritional Information: 90 calories, 1g protein, 2g carbohydrates, 9g fat, 1g fiber, 2mg cholesterol, 370mg sodium, 30mg potassium.

Instant Muhammara

Yield: 4 servings | Prep time: 10 minutes | Cook time: 10 minutes

Ingredients:

- 1 cup roasted red bell peppers (from a jar or freshly roasted)
- 1/2 cup walnuts, toasted
- 1/3 cup fresh breadcrumbs
- 2 garlic cloves, minced
- 1 tablespoon lemon juice
- 1 tablespoon pomegranate molasses (or substitute with maple syrup)
- 1 teaspoon ground cumin
- 1/4 teaspoon cayenne pepper (adjust to taste)
- 1/4 cup extra virgin olive oil
- Salt to taste

Directions:

1. Set the Instant Pot to the sauté setting. Lightly toast the walnuts for 2-3 minutes or until they become fragrant. Remove and set aside.
2. In the Instant Pot (turned off), combine the roasted red bell peppers, toasted walnuts, breadcrumbs, garlic, lemon juice, pomegranate molasses, cumin, and cayenne pepper.
3. Using an immersion blender, blend the mixture until smooth. If you don't have an immersion blender, you can transfer the mixture to a regular blender.
4. With the blender running, slowly add the olive oil until well combined. Season with salt to taste.

Nutritional Information: 240 calories, 4g protein, 12g carbohydrates, 20g fat, 3g fiber, 0mg cholesterol, 180mg sodium, 180mg potassium.

Mediterranean Pesto Sauce

Yield: 4 servings | Prep time: 15 minutes | Cook time: 5 minutes

Ingredients:

- 2 cups fresh basil leaves, packed
- 1 cup fresh parsley, packed
- 1/2 cup sun-dried tomatoes (soaked in warm water for 10 minutes if not oil-packed)
- 1/4 cup toasted pine nuts
- 2 garlic cloves, minced
- 1/2 cup grated Parmesan cheese
- 1/4 cup crumbled feta cheese
- 1/2 cup extra virgin olive oil
- 1 tablespoon lemon juice
- Salt and pepper to taste

Directions:

1. Using the sauté function of the Instant Pot, lightly toast the pine nuts for 2-3 minutes or until golden brown. Remove and set aside.
2. Combine basil, parsley, sun-dried tomatoes, toasted pine nuts, garlic, Parmesan, and feta in the pot (turned off).
3. Using an immersion blender, process the ingredients until smooth. If you don't have an immersion blender, you can transfer the mixture to a regular blender.
4. Gradually blend in the olive oil and lemon juice until smooth. Season with salt and pepper to taste.

Nutritional Information: 380 calories, 8g protein, 8g carbohydrates, 36g fat, 3g fiber, 20mg cholesterol, 300mg sodium, 250mg potassium.

Whipped Feta with Roasted Peppers

Yield: 4 servings | Prep time: 10 minutes | Cook time: 15 minutes

Ingredients:

- 1 cup feta cheese, crumbled
- 1/4 cup cream cheese, softened
- 2 red bell peppers
- 2 garlic cloves, minced
- 2 tablespoons extra virgin olive oil
- 1 tablespoon lemon juice
- 1/4 teaspoon smoked paprika (optional)
- Salt and pepper to taste
- Fresh parsley for garnish

Directions:

1. Place red bell peppers on the trivet inside the Instant Pot. Add 1 cup of water to the pot. Seal and set the pot to 'Steam' for 7 minutes.
2. Once done, perform a quick release and carefully remove peppers. Allow them to cool slightly and then peel the skin and remove seeds. Roughly chop the roasted peppers.
3. In the Instant Pot (emptied and turned off), combine feta cheese, cream cheese, chopped roasted peppers, garlic, olive oil, and lemon juice.
4. Use an immersion blender to blend the mixture until smooth and creamy. Season with salt, pepper, and smoked paprika.
5. Transfer to a serving dish and garnish with fresh parsley. Serve with pita or fresh crusty bread.

Nutritional Information: 250 calories, 7g protein, 8g carbohydrates, 20g fat, 2g fiber, 45mg cholesterol, 520mg sodium, 180mg potassium.

Quick & Creamy Hummus

Yield: 4 servings | Prep time: 10 minutes | Cook time: 0 minutes (no cooking required)

Ingredients:

- 1 can (15 oz) chickpeas, drained and rinsed
- 3 garlic cloves
- 1/4 cup tahini
- 3 tablespoons lemon juice
- 2 tablespoons extra virgin olive oil
- 1/4 teaspoon ground cumin
- Salt and pepper to taste
- 2-4 tablespoons water, as needed
- Paprika and extra olive oil for garnish

Directions:

1. In the Instant Pot, combine chickpeas, garlic, tahini, lemon juice, olive oil, ground cumin, salt, and pepper.
2. Using an immersion blender, blend until the mixture is smooth. If it's too thick, gradually add water until you reach your desired consistency.
3. Taste and adjust seasoning if needed.
4. Transfer hummus to a serving bowl. Drizzle with a bit more olive oil and sprinkle with paprika before serving.
5. Serve with fresh veggies, pita, or crackers.

Nutritional Information: 280 calories, 9g protein, 24g carbohydrates, 18g fat, 7g fiber, 0mg cholesterol, 300mg sodium, 240mg potassium.

Spiced Tomato & Almond Dip

Yield: 4 servings | Prep time: 10 minutes | Cook time: 15 minutes

Ingredients:

- 1 cup roasted almonds
- 2 large tomatoes, diced
- 2 garlic cloves, minced
- 2 tablespoons olive oil
- 1 teaspoon smoked paprika
- 1/2 teaspoon ground cumin
- 1/4 teaspoon cayenne pepper (adjust based on heat preference)
- Salt to taste
- 2 tablespoons fresh parsley, chopped
- 1 tablespoon lemon juice

Directions:

1. Turn on the Instant Pot's sauté mode. Add olive oil, minced garlic, and spices. Sauté for about 2 minutes until fragrant.
2. Add the diced tomatoes to the pot and sauté for another 8-10 minutes until they are softened and most of the liquid has evaporated.
3. Turn off the Instant Pot and let the tomato mixture cool for a few minutes.
4. In a blender or food processor, combine the tomato mixture, roasted almonds, lemon juice, and parsley. Blend until smooth, adjusting salt if needed.
5. Transfer to a serving bowl and garnish with a sprinkle of smoked paprika and a drizzle of olive oil. Serve with toasted pita or fresh vegetables.

Nutritional Information: 230 calories, 6g protein, 12g carbohydrates, 18g fat, 4g fiber, 0mg cholesterol, 90mg sodium, 380mg potassium.

Classic Mediterranean Salads

Pressure-Cooked Potato Salad

Yield: 4 servings | Prep time: 15 minutes | Cook time: 10 minutes

Ingredients:

- 1.5 lbs small potatoes, halved or quartered based on size
- 1 cup water
- 1/2 cup kalamata olives, pitted and sliced
- 1/4 cup red onion, finely chopped
- 1/4 cup fresh parsley, chopped
- 1/4 cup olive oil
- 2 tablespoons lemon juice
- 1 garlic clove, minced
- Salt and black pepper to taste
- 1/2 cup crumbled feta cheese (optional)

Directions:

1. Add potatoes and water to the Instant Pot. Seal the lid, ensuring the vent is set to "Sealing". Use the Manual or Pressure Cook setting on High for 5 minutes.
2. Once the cooking time has finished, do a quick release by moving the vent to "Venting". Once all the pressure is released, open the lid and drain the potatoes.
3. In a large bowl, whisk together olive oil, lemon juice, minced garlic, salt, and black pepper.
4. Add the drained potatoes, kalamata olives, red onion, and parsley to the bowl and gently toss to combine. If desired, sprinkle crumbled feta cheese on top.
5. Allow the salad to cool for a bit and serve either warm or refrigerate for later use.

Nutritional Information: 280 calories, 5g protein, 30g carbohydrates, 15g fat, 4g fiber, 10mg cholesterol, 360mg sodium, 720mg potassium.

Quick Couscous & Vegetable Salad

Yield: 4 servings | Prep time: 10 minutes | Cook time: 5 minutes

Ingredients:

- 1 cup couscous
- 1 1/4 cups water
- 1 cup cherry tomatoes, halved
- 1 cucumber, diced
- 1/2 red bell pepper, diced
- 1/4 cup red onion, finely chopped
- 1/4 cup fresh parsley, chopped
- 1/4 cup fresh mint, chopped
- 1/4 cup kalamata olives, pitted and sliced
- 1/4 cup feta cheese, crumbled
- 2 tablespoons olive oil
- 2 tablespoons lemon juice
- Salt and pepper to taste

Directions:

1. Add water to the Instant Pot and place the trivet inside. In a separate, heat-proof bowl, add couscous. Place the bowl on the trivet. Seal the lid and set the Instant Pot to Steam mode for 5 minutes.
2. After the cooking time is complete, release the pressure manually. Carefully remove the bowl and fluff the couscous with a fork. Allow it to cool slightly.
3. In a large bowl, combine cherry tomatoes, cucumber, red bell pepper, red onion, parsley, mint, and olives.
4. Add the cooled couscous to the vegetable mixture. Drizzle with olive oil and lemon juice, and season with salt and pepper. Gently mix to combine.
5. Top with crumbled feta cheese before serving.

Nutritional Information: 290 calories, 8g protein, 45g carbohydrates, 9g fat, 3g fiber, 8mg cholesterol, 240mg sodium, 330mg potassium.

Instant Pot Tabouleh

Yield: 4 servings | Prep time: 15 minutes | Cook time: 5 minutes

Ingredients:

- 1/2 cup bulgur wheat
- 1 cup water
- 1 cup fresh parsley, finely chopped
- 1/2 cup fresh mint, finely chopped
- 4 green onions, finely sliced
- 1 cucumber, diced
- 2 ripe tomatoes, diced
- 3 tablespoons olive oil
- 3 tablespoons fresh lemon juice
- Salt and pepper to taste

Directions:

1. Add water to the Instant Pot and place the trivet inside. In a separate, heat-proof bowl, add bulgur wheat. Place the bowl on the trivet. Seal the lid and set the Instant Pot to High Pressure mode for 5 minutes.
2. After the cooking time is complete, allow for a natural release for 10 minutes, then release any remaining pressure. Carefully remove the bowl and fluff the bulgur with a fork. Transfer to a large bowl and let it cool to room temperature.
3. Once cooled, add the parsley, mint, green onions, cucumber, and tomatoes to the bulgur.
4. In a separate bowl, whisk together the olive oil, lemon juice, salt, and pepper. Pour this dressing over the bulgur mixture and toss to combine.
5. Refrigerate for at least one hour before serving to allow flavors to meld.

Nutritional Information: 220 calories, 6g protein, 31g carbohydrates, 9g fat, 6g fiber, 0mg cholesterol, 50mg sodium, 400mg potassium.

Chickpea & Roasted Pepper Salad

Yield: 4 servings | Prep time: 10 minutes | Cook time: 10 minutes

Ingredients:

- 1 cup dried chickpeas, soaked overnight
- 4 cups water
- 2 roasted red peppers, diced
- 1/4 cup red onion, finely chopped
- 1/4 cup fresh parsley, chopped
- 2 tablespoons olive oil
- 1 tablespoon balsamic vinegar
- 1 garlic clove, minced
- Salt and pepper to taste
- 1 teaspoon cumin (optional)

Directions:

1. Rinse the soaked chickpeas and add them to the Instant Pot with the water. Set to High Pressure mode for 10 minutes.
2. Once cooked, allow for a natural pressure release. Drain the chickpeas and let them cool.
3. In a large bowl, combine the cooled chickpeas, roasted red peppers, red onion, and parsley.
4. In a small bowl, whisk together the olive oil, balsamic vinegar, minced garlic, salt, pepper, and cumin if using. Pour the dressing over the chickpea mixture and toss to combine.
5. Serve immediately or refrigerate to let the flavors meld.

Nutritional Information: 290 calories, 11g protein, 40g carbohydrates, 10g fat, 10g fiber, 0mg cholesterol, 80mg sodium, 520mg potassium.

Mediterranean Beet Salad

Yield: 4 servings | Prep time: 15 minutes | Cook time: 25 minutes

Ingredients:

- 4 medium-sized beets, washed and trimmed
- 4 cups water
- 1/2 cup crumbled feta cheese
- 1/4 cup fresh parsley, finely chopped
- 1/4 cup fresh mint, finely chopped
- 1/4 cup red onion, finely diced
- 2 tablespoons olive oil
- 2 tablespoons balsamic vinegar
- 1 tablespoon lemon juice
- Salt and black pepper to taste
- 1/4 cup chopped walnuts (optional)

Directions:

1. Add beets and water to the Instant Pot. Close the lid and set to High Pressure for 25 minutes. Once done, quick release the pressure and carefully open the lid.
2. Remove the beets from the pot and run them under cold water. Once cool enough to handle, peel and dice them.
3. In a large mixing bowl, combine diced beets, feta cheese, parsley, mint, and red onion.
4. In a separate bowl, whisk together the olive oil, balsamic vinegar, lemon juice, salt, and pepper. Pour over the beet mixture and toss to coat.
5. Garnish with chopped walnuts if using. Serve chilled.

Nutritional Information: 210 calories, 7g protein, 24g carbohydrates, 11g fat, 5g fiber, 15mg cholesterol, 290mg sodium, 540mg potassium.

Fennel & Citrus Medley

Yield: 4 servings | Prep time: 15 minutes | Cook time: 5 minutes

Ingredients:

- 2 large fennel bulbs, thinly sliced
- 1 orange, peeled and segmented
- 1 grapefruit, peeled and segmented
- 1 lemon, zested and juiced
- 2 tablespoons olive oil
- 1 tablespoon honey or agave nectar
- Salt and black pepper to taste
- 1/4 cup fresh mint leaves, roughly chopped
- 2 tablespoons pine nuts (optional)

Directions:

1. In the Instant Pot, select the "Sauté" function. Add the olive oil, fennel slices, and sauté for about 3-4 minutes until they start to soften.
2. In a large mixing bowl, combine the sautéed fennel, orange segments, and grapefruit segments.
3. In a small bowl, whisk together lemon zest, lemon juice, honey, salt, and pepper. Pour over the fennel and citrus mixture and toss to coat evenly.
4. Serve the medley in individual dishes or a large salad bowl, garnished with fresh mint leaves and pine nuts if using.

Nutritional Information: 180 calories, 3g protein, 27g carbohydrates, 7g fat, 6g fiber, 0mg cholesterol, 60mg sodium, 520mg potassium.

Warm Lentil & Herb Salad

Yield: 4 servings | Prep time: 10 minutes | Cook time: 15 minutes

Ingredients:

- 1 cup green lentils, rinsed and drained
- 2.5 cups vegetable broth or water
- 1/2 cup fresh parsley, finely chopped
- 1/4 cup fresh mint, finely chopped
- 1/4 cup fresh cilantro, finely chopped
- 1 medium red onion, finely diced
- 1/4 cup olive oil
- Juice of 1 lemon
- 2 garlic cloves, minced
- Salt and black pepper to taste
- 1/4 cup feta cheese crumbles (optional)
- 1/4 cup pitted Kalamata olives, halved

Directions:

1. Add lentils and vegetable broth or water to the Instant Pot. Close the lid and set to "Manual" or "Pressure Cook" on high for 15 minutes.
2. Once done, allow the pressure to release naturally. Drain any excess liquid if necessary.
3. While lentils are still warm, transfer them to a large mixing bowl. Add the red onion, parsley, mint, cilantro, olive oil, lemon juice, garlic, salt, and black pepper. Mix until well combined.
4. Serve in individual dishes or a large salad bowl, garnished with feta cheese crumbles and Kalamata olives if using.

Nutritional Information: 350 calories, 18g protein, 40g carbohydrates, 14g fat, 16g fiber, 5mg cholesterol (if using feta), 350mg sodium, 600mg potassium.

Tomato, Mozzarella & Basil Salad

Yield: 4 servings | Prep time: 10 minutes | Cook time: 0 minutes

Ingredients:

- 4 large ripe tomatoes, sliced
- 200g fresh mozzarella cheese, sliced
- 1/4 cup fresh basil leaves
- 3 tablespoons extra-virgin olive oil
- 2 tablespoons balsamic vinegar
- Salt and freshly ground black pepper, to taste
- 1 clove garlic, minced (optional)
- 1/4 teaspoon red pepper flakes (optional)

Directions:

1. Arrange tomato and mozzarella slices on a platter, alternating and overlapping them.
2. Sprinkle with fresh basil leaves, torn if large.
3. In a small bowl, whisk together olive oil, balsamic vinegar, minced garlic (if using), and red pepper flakes. Season with salt and black pepper.
4. Drizzle the dressing over the tomato and mozzarella slices just before serving.

Nutritional Information: 220 calories, 10g protein, 8g carbohydrates, 16g fat, 2g fiber, 25mg cholesterol, 150mg sodium, 400mg potassium.

Orzo & Spinach Salad

Yield: 4 servings | Prep time: 10 minutes | Cook time: 5 minutes

Ingredients:

- 1 cup uncooked orzo pasta
- 2 cups fresh spinach, chopped
- 1/2 cup cherry tomatoes, halved
- 1/4 cup feta cheese, crumbled
- 1/4 cup black olives, sliced
- 3 tablespoons extra-virgin olive oil
- 2 tablespoons fresh lemon juice
- 1 clove garlic, minced
- Salt and freshly ground black pepper, to taste
- 1 tablespoon fresh oregano, chopped (or 1 teaspoon dried oregano)

Directions:

1. Add 4 cups of water to the Instant Pot and insert the steamer basket. Place the orzo in the basket. Lock the lid in place and set the steam release handle to "Sealing." Cook on manual high pressure for 5 minutes.
2. Once the cooking cycle is done, do a quick release of the steam. Remove the orzo and rinse under cold water to cool. Drain well.
3. In a large bowl, combine cooled orzo, spinach, cherry tomatoes, feta cheese, and olives.
4. In a separate small bowl, whisk together olive oil, lemon juice, garlic, salt, pepper, and oregano. Pour dressing over the salad and toss to combine.

Nutritional Information: 320 calories, 9g protein, 42g carbohydrates, 14g fat, 3g fiber, 10mg cholesterol, 270mg sodium, 310mg potassium.

Pressure-Cooked Artichoke Salad

Yield: 4 servings | Prep time: 10 minutes | Cook time: 15 minutes

Ingredients:

- 4 medium-sized artichokes, cleaned and quartered
- 1 lemon, juiced
- 1/4 cup extra-virgin olive oil
- 2 garlic cloves, minced
- 1/2 cup cherry tomatoes, halved
- 1/4 cup Kalamata olives, pitted and sliced
- 1/4 cup fresh parsley, finely chopped
- Salt and freshly ground black pepper, to taste
- 1/4 cup crumbled feta cheese (optional)

Directions:

1. Place the cleaned and quartered artichokes in the Instant Pot. Add enough water just to cover the artichokes and add half of the lemon juice.
2. Close the Instant Pot lid and set the valve to "Sealing." Cook on manual high pressure for 15 minutes. Once done, release pressure immediately and open the lid.
3. Drain the artichokes and let them cool. Once cool, transfer them to a large mixing bowl.
4. Add olive oil, remaining lemon juice, garlic, cherry tomatoes, olives, parsley, salt, and pepper to the bowl. Mix gently until well combined. Top with crumbled feta cheese if desired before serving.

Nutritional Information: 220 calories, 5g protein, 18g carbohydrates, 15g fat, 7g fiber, 10mg cholesterol, 330mg sodium, 420mg potassium.

Delightful Desserts

Instant Pot Flan

Yield: 4 servings | Prep time: 10 minutes | Cook time: 25 minutes

Ingredients:

- 1 cup granulated sugar
- 1/4 cup water
- 3 large eggs
- 1 can (12 oz.) evaporated milk
- 1 teaspoon vanilla extract
- A pinch of salt
- Fresh berries or fruit slices for garnish (optional)

Directions:

1. In a saucepan over medium heat, combine sugar and water. Stir constantly until the sugar dissolves and becomes a golden caramel color. Pour this caramel into four ramekins, tilting each to coat the bottom evenly.
2. In a mixing bowl, whisk together eggs, evaporated milk, vanilla extract, and salt. Pour this mixture over the caramel in each ramekin.
3. Pour 1 cup of water into the Instant Pot. Place the trivet inside, and then set the ramekins on top. Close the lid and set the valve to "Sealing." Cook on manual high pressure for 12 minutes. Allow the pressure to release naturally for 10 minutes, then quick release any remaining pressure.
4. Remove ramekins, let them cool to room temperature, and then refrigerate for at least 2 hours. When ready to serve, run a knife around the edge of each flan to loosen, invert onto a plate, and garnish with fresh berries or fruit slices if desired.

Nutritional Information: 290 calories, 8g protein, 45g carbohydrates, 10g fat, 0g fiber, 165mg cholesterol, 130mg sodium, 290mg potassium.

Pressure-Cooked Rice Pudding

Yield: 4 servings | Prep time: 5 minutes | Cook time: 25 minutes

Ingredients:

- 1 cup Arborio rice
- 4 cups whole milk
- 1/2 cup granulated sugar
- 1 teaspoon pure vanilla extract
- 1/2 teaspoon ground cinnamon
- 1/4 teaspoon salt
- Zest of 1 lemon
- Raisins or fresh berries for garnish (optional)

Directions:

1. Add the Arborio rice, milk, sugar, vanilla extract, cinnamon, salt, and lemon zest to the Instant Pot and stir to combine.
2. Close the lid, set the valve to "Sealing," and cook on the Porridge setting or manual high pressure for 20 minutes.
3. Allow the pressure to release naturally for 10 minutes, then quick release any remaining pressure.
4. Stir the rice pudding thoroughly, ensuring it has a creamy consistency. If it's too thick, you can add a little more milk to achieve your desired texture. Serve warm, garnished with raisins or fresh berries if desired.

Nutritional Information: 320 calories, 8g protein, 58g carbohydrates, 7g fat, 1g fiber, 20mg cholesterol, 190mg sodium, 330mg potassium.

Mediterranean Cheesecake
Yield: 6 servings | Prep time: 15 minutes | Cook time: 40 minutes

Ingredients:

- 1 cup almond flour (for crust)
- 3 tablespoons olive oil (for crust)
- 1/4 teaspoon salt (for crust)
- 2 cups ricotta cheese
- 1/2 cup honey
- 1 teaspoon vanilla extract
- Zest of 1 lemon
- 3 large eggs
- 1/4 cup slivered almonds (optional for garnish)
- Fresh figs or berries (for garnish)

Directions:

1. In a bowl, mix almond flour, olive oil, and salt to form a crumbly dough. Press this mixture into the bottom of a springform pan that fits into your Instant Pot.
2. In another bowl, whisk together the ricotta cheese, honey, vanilla extract, lemon zest, and eggs until smooth. Pour this mixture over the almond crust in the springform pan.
3. Add 1 cup of water to the Instant Pot. Place the springform pan on the trivet and carefully lower it into the Instant Pot. Close the lid, set the valve to "Sealing," and cook on manual high pressure for 35 minutes.
4. Allow the pressure to release naturally. Once released, remove the cheesecake and let it cool to room temperature. Once cooled, refrigerate for at least 4 hours, preferably overnight.
5. Before serving, garnish with slivered almonds and fresh figs or berries.

Nutritional Information: 410 calories, 15g protein, 32g carbohydrates, 25g fat, 2g fiber, 125mg cholesterol, 180mg sodium, 210mg potassium.

Quick Poached Pears in Wine
Yield: 4 servings | Prep time: 10 minutes | Cook time: 8 minutes

Ingredients:

- 4 ripe but firm pears, peeled, halved, and cored
- 2 cups red wine (such as a Cabernet or Merlot)
- 1/2 cup honey
- 1 cinnamon stick
- 2-star anise
- Zest of 1 orange
- Fresh mint leaves (for garnish)

Directions:

1. In the Instant Pot, combine the wine, honey, cinnamon stick, star anise, and orange zest.
2. Gently place the pear halves into the wine mixture, ensuring they are submerged.
3. Lock the Instant Pot lid in place and set the valve to "Sealing". Select the "Manual" setting and adjust the time to 8 minutes on high pressure.
4. Once the cooking cycle is complete, allow the pressure to release naturally for about 10 minutes, then do a quick release. Carefully remove the pears and set them aside.
5. Serve the poached pears in individual bowls with some of the wine reduction poured over. Garnish with fresh mint leaves.

Nutritional Information: 260 calories, 1g protein, 62g carbohydrates, 0.5g fat, 5g fiber, 0mg cholesterol, 10mg sodium, 210mg potassium.

Olive Oil & Lemon Cake

Yield: 6 servings | Prep time: 15 minutes | Cook time: 40 minutes

Ingredients:

- 1 cup all-purpose flour
- 3/4 cup granulated sugar
- 1/4 cup extra virgin olive oil
- 3 large eggs
- Zest of 2 lemons
- 2 tablespoons fresh lemon juice
- 1 teaspoon baking powder
- 1/4 teaspoon salt
- 1 cup water (for Instant Pot)
- Powdered sugar for dusting (optional)

Directions:

1. In a large bowl, whisk together the eggs and sugar until pale and slightly thickened. Gradually whisk in the olive oil, lemon zest, and lemon juice.
2. In a separate bowl, sift together the flour, baking powder, and salt. Gently fold the dry ingredients into the wet ingredients until just combined.
3. Pour the batter into a greased 7-inch springform pan that fits into your Instant Pot. Cover the pan with aluminum foil.
4. Pour 1 cup of water into the Instant Pot and place the trivet inside. Carefully lower the pan onto the trivet using a sling or long-handled tongs.
5. Lock the Instant Pot lid in place and set the valve to "Sealing". Select the "Manual" setting and adjust the time to 40 minutes on high pressure. Once the cooking cycle is complete, let it naturally release for about 10 minutes, then do a quick release. Remove the cake, let it cool, then dust with powdered sugar if desired.

Nutritional Information: 280 calories, 5g protein, 44g carbohydrates, 10g fat, 1g fiber, 95mg cholesterol, 150mg sodium, 80mg potassium.

Almond & Fig Tart

Yield: 6 servings | Prep time: 20 minutes | Cook time: 35 minutes

Ingredients:

- 1 pre-made pie crust (or homemade if you prefer)
- 1 cup almond flour
- 1/2 cup granulated sugar
- 6 fresh figs, quartered
- 1/2 cup almonds, roughly chopped
- 1/4 cup honey
- 1 teaspoon vanilla extract
- 1/2 teaspoon almond extract
- 1 large egg
- 1/4 teaspoon salt
- 1 cup water (for Instant Pot)

Directions:

1. In a medium bowl, mix together almond flour, sugar, egg, honey, vanilla extract, almond extract, and salt until it forms a smooth paste.
2. Roll out the pie crust into a 7-inch tart pan that fits into your Instant Pot. Spread the almond paste mixture evenly over the pie crust.
3. Place the quartered figs on top of the almond mixture and sprinkle with chopped almonds.
4. Cover the tart pan with aluminum foil. Pour 1 cup of water into the Instant Pot and place the trivet inside. Carefully place the tart pan onto the trivet.
5. Lock the Instant Pot lid in place and set the valve to "Sealing". Select the "Manual" setting and adjust the time to 35 minutes on high pressure. Once done, allow it to naturally release for 10 minutes, then perform a quick release. Carefully remove the tart, let it cool, then serve.

Nutritional Information: 325 calories, 6g protein, 42g carbohydrates, 16g fat, 4g fiber, 35mg cholesterol, 125mg sodium, 190mg potassium.

Instant Pot Baklava Pudding
Yield: 4 servings | Prep time: 15 minutes | Cook time: 20 minutes

Ingredients:

- 1 cup rice, rinsed
- 2 1/2 cups almond milk (or any preferred milk)
- 1/2 cup honey
- 1/4 cup chopped walnuts
- 1/4 cup chopped pistachios
- 1 teaspoon vanilla extract
- 1 teaspoon ground cinnamon
- 1/4 teaspoon ground cloves
- 1/4 teaspoon salt
- 1 tablespoon unsalted butter
- 1/2 teaspoon grated lemon zest
- 1 cup water (for Instant Pot)

Directions:

1. In the Instant Pot, combine rice, almond milk, honey, vanilla extract, cinnamon, cloves, and salt. Stir to ensure even mixing.
2. Secure the lid and set the Instant Pot to the "Porridge" setting. Adjust the cooking time to 20 minutes on low pressure.
3. Once the cooking is complete, allow a natural pressure release for 10 minutes, followed by a quick release.
4. Stir in unsalted butter and lemon zest until the butter is melted. Pour the pudding into serving dishes, and while it's still warm, garnish with chopped walnuts and pistachios.
5. Let it cool a bit before serving. For best results, you can refrigerate for 1-2 hours to get a thicker consistency.

Nutritional Information: 320 calories, 5g protein, 60g carbohydrates, 9g fat, 2g fiber, 8mg cholesterol, 110mg sodium, 160mg potassium.

Creamy Orange & Chocolate Pots
Yield: 4 servings | Prep time: 10 minutes | Cook time: 30 minutes

Ingredients:

- 2 cups full-fat coconut milk
- Zest and juice of 1 orange
- 1/2 cup dark chocolate (70% cocoa or higher), chopped
- 1/4 cup honey or maple syrup
- 1 teaspoon pure vanilla extract
- A pinch of sea salt
- 1 tablespoon chia seeds (optional for extra thickness)
- Fresh orange slices for garnish

Directions:

1. In the Instant Pot, combine coconut milk, orange zest, and juice, ensuring a smooth mixture without lumps.
2. Add the chopped dark chocolate to the mixture and gently stir. Close the Instant Pot lid and set it to the "Slow Cook" mode for 30 minutes.
3. Once the cooking time is over, whisk in honey or maple syrup, vanilla extract, and a pinch of sea salt. If using chia seeds for added thickness, stir them in now.
4. Allow the mixture to cool for a few minutes inside the pot. Once slightly cooled, pour into individual serving pots or glasses.
5. Chill in the refrigerator for at least 2 hours or until set. Garnish with fresh orange slices before serving.

Nutritional Information: 420 calories, 4g protein, 32g carbohydrates, 31g fat, 5g fiber, 0mg cholesterol, 40mg sodium, 290mg potassium.

Pistachio & Honey Crème Brûlée

Yield: 4 servings | Prep time: 15 minutes | Cook time: 25 minutes

Ingredients:

- 2 cups heavy cream
- 1/4 cup honey
- 1 vanilla bean, split and seeds scraped (or 1 tsp vanilla extract)
- 5 large egg yolks
- 1/4 cup unsalted pistachios, finely chopped
- 4 tablespoons granulated sugar, for topping
- 2 tablespoons crushed pistachios, for garnish

Directions:

1. In a medium saucepan, heat the heavy cream, honey, and vanilla (both the bean and seeds) over medium heat until it begins to simmer. Once simmering, remove from heat and let it steep for 5 minutes.
2. In a separate bowl, whisk the egg yolks. Slowly pour the warm cream mixture into the egg yolks, whisking constantly to ensure the eggs don't scramble.
3. Stir in the finely chopped pistachios. Divide the mixture equally among 4 ramekins.
4. Pour 1 cup of water into the Instant Pot and place the trivet inside. Arrange the ramekins on the trivet. Secure the lid and set the Instant Pot to "High Pressure" for 7 minutes. Once done, allow a natural release.
5. Remove ramekins from the Instant Pot and let them cool to room temperature. Refrigerate for at least 4 hours, or until set. Before serving, sprinkle each ramekin with 1 tablespoon of sugar and use a kitchen torch to caramelize the sugar. Garnish with crushed pistachios.

Nutritional Information: 520 calories, 7g protein, 28g carbohydrates, 42g fat, 1g fiber, 310mg cholesterol, 40mg sodium, 160mg potassium.

Quick Berry & Mascarpone Delight

Yield: 4 servings | Prep time: 10 minutes | Cook time: 1 minute

Ingredients:

- 1 cup mixed berries (blueberries, raspberries, strawberries)
- 1 cup mascarpone cheese
- 1/4 cup honey or agave syrup
- 1 tsp vanilla extract
- Zest of 1 lemon
- 1/4 cup crushed almond biscotti or graham crackers (for garnish)
- Mint leaves (for garnish)

Directions:

1. In a mixing bowl, combine mascarpone cheese, honey, vanilla extract, and lemon zest. Mix until well blended.
2. Pour 1 cup of water into the Instant Pot and place the trivet inside. Place the mixing bowl with the mascarpone mixture on the trivet. Secure the lid and set the Instant Pot to "Steam" mode for just 1 minute.
3. Quick release the pressure and carefully remove the bowl from the Instant Pot. Let it cool for a few minutes.
4. Spoon the mascarpone mixture into individual serving glasses or bowls. Top with mixed berries and sprinkle with crushed almond biscotti or graham crackers.
5. Garnish with a mint leaf and serve chilled.

Nutritional Information: 320 calories, 5g protein, 25g carbohydrates, 23g fat, 2g fiber, 65mg cholesterol, 40mg sodium, 90mg potassium.

Dairy & Cheese Magic

Instant Pot Feta & Spinach Dip

Yield: 4 servings | Prep time: 10 minutes | Cook time: 5 minutes

Ingredients:

- 1 cup crumbled feta cheese
- 2 cups fresh spinach, roughly chopped
- 1/4 cup plain Greek yogurt
- 2 cloves garlic, minced
- 1 tablespoon olive oil
- 1/2 teaspoon dried oregano
- 1/4 teaspoon black pepper
- Red pepper flakes, to taste (optional)
- Lemon zest from 1 lemon

Directions:

1. Turn the Instant Pot to the "Sauté" mode and heat the olive oil. Add garlic and sauté until fragrant.
2. Add spinach to the pot and sauté until wilted, about 2 minutes.
3. Add feta cheese, Greek yogurt, dried oregano, black pepper, and red pepper flakes (if using). Mix well.
4. Secure the lid, set the Instant Pot to "Manual" mode, and cook for 3 minutes.
5. Quick release the pressure, stir in lemon zest, and serve warm with pita bread or vegetable sticks.

Nutritional Information: 180 calories, 8g protein, 6g carbohydrates, 14g fat, 1g fiber, 35mg cholesterol, 320mg sodium, 180mg potassium.

Creamy Ricotta in Minutes

Yield: 4 servings | Prep time: 5 minutes | Cook time: 10 minutes

Ingredients:

- 4 cups whole milk
- 1 cup heavy cream
- 3 tablespoons white vinegar or lemon juice
- 1/2 teaspoon salt

Directions:

1. In the Instant Pot, combine whole milk and heavy cream. Press the "Sauté" button and warm the mixture until it reaches about 190°F (just before boiling), stirring occasionally to prevent burning.
2. Turn off the Instant Pot. Add the white vinegar or lemon juice and gently stir the mixture for a minute. The milk should begin to curdle immediately.
3. Let the mixture sit for about 5 minutes to allow curds to fully form.
4. Using a slotted spoon, transfer the curds to a cheesecloth-lined colander placed over a bowl. Allow it to drain for about 5 minutes for a creamier texture. For a firmer ricotta, let it drain longer.
5. Transfer to a bowl, sprinkle with salt, and stir gently.

Nutritional Information: 280 calories, 14g protein, 8g carbohydrates, 22g fat, 0g fiber, 105mg cholesterol, 360mg sodium, 320mg potassium.

Mediterranean Queso Fundido

Yield: 4 servings | Prep time: 10 minutes | Cook time: 15 minutes

Ingredients:

- 2 cups shredded mozzarella cheese
- 1 cup feta cheese, crumbled
- 1/2 cup diced sun-dried tomatoes in oil, drained
- 1/4 cup chopped Kalamata olives
- 1/4 cup diced roasted red bell peppers
- 2 cloves garlic, minced
- 1 tablespoon olive oil
- 1/2 teaspoon dried oregano
- Fresh parsley, chopped (for garnish)
- Pita chips or bread, for serving

Directions:

1. Turn on the Instant Pot to "Sauté" mode. Add olive oil and minced garlic, sautéing until aromatic.
2. Add the sun-dried tomatoes, Kalamata olives, and roasted red bell peppers to the pot and sauté for another 2 minutes.
3. Sprinkle in the mozzarella and feta cheeses, stirring continuously until melted and well combined.
4. Once the cheese is fully melted, turn off the Instant Pot. Mix in the dried oregano and transfer the queso fundido to a serving dish.
5. Garnish with fresh parsley. Serve warm with pita chips or bread.

Nutritional Information: 340 calories, 17g protein, 10g carbohydrates, 26g fat, 2g fiber, 80mg cholesterol, 730mg sodium, 220mg potassium.

Quick Mozzarella & Tomato Melt

Yield: 4 servings | Prep time: 5 minutes | Cook time: 10 minutes

Ingredients:

- 8 slices of whole grain bread
- 2 large tomatoes, sliced
- 1 cup fresh mozzarella cheese, sliced
- 1/4 cup fresh basil leaves
- 1 tablespoon olive oil
- 1 clove garlic, minced
- Salt and pepper, to taste
- Balsamic glaze or reduction (optional, for drizzling)

Directions:

1. In the Instant Pot, select the "Sauté" mode and heat olive oil. Once hot, add the minced garlic and sauté for about 30 seconds until fragrant.
2. Place 4 slices of bread in the pot and layer each slice with mozzarella slices, tomato slices, and a sprinkle of salt and pepper. Top each with another slice of bread.
3. Close the Instant Pot lid, set the valve to "Venting", and select the "Warm" mode. Let the sandwiches heat for 5 minutes or until the cheese starts to melt.
4. Carefully open the lid, flip the sandwiches, and let them heat for another 3-4 minutes or until the bread is toasted and the cheese is fully melted.
5. Serve hot, drizzled with balsamic glaze and garnished with fresh basil leaves.

Nutritional Information: 290 calories, 15g protein, 30g carbohydrates, 12g fat, 4g fiber, 30mg cholesterol, 340mg sodium, 210mg potassium.

Labneh with Olive Oil & Za'atar

Yield: 4 servings | Prep time: 10 minutes | Cook time: 8 hours (mostly passive time for straining)

Ingredients:

- 4 cups full-fat plain Greek yogurt
- 1 teaspoon salt
- 2 tablespoons olive oil (extra virgin)
- 1 tablespoon za'atar spice mix
- Optional: Fresh herbs for garnish (like mint or parsley)
- Optional: Sliced olives or halved cherry tomatoes

Directions:

1. Mix the Greek yogurt and salt in a bowl until well combined.
2. Line a fine-mesh sieve with 2 layers of cheesecloth and place it over a large bowl. Pour the yogurt mixture into the sieve, fold the cheesecloth over the top, and place a heavy object (like a can) on top to help strain the liquid.
3. Allow the yogurt to strain in the refrigerator for at least 8 hours, or overnight. This will thicken the yogurt and turn it into labneh.
4. Once strained, transfer the thickened labneh to a serving dish. Using the back of a spoon, create a well in the center of the labneh and pour in the olive oil. Sprinkle za'atar and optional herbs, olives, or tomatoes on top.
5. Serve with warm pita bread or vegetable sticks.

Nutritional Information: 190 calories, 15g protein, 8g carbohydrates, 11g fat, 0.5g fiber, 10mg cholesterol, 650mg sodium, 260mg potassium.

Pressure-Cooked Cheese Fondue

Yield: 4 servings | Prep time: 10 minutes | Cook time: 6 minutes

Ingredients:

- 200g Gruyere cheese, grated
- 200g Emmental cheese, grated
- 1 cup dry white wine (such as a Sauvignon Blanc or any Mediterranean variety)
- 1 garlic clove, halved
- 1 teaspoon lemon juice
- 1 tablespoon cornstarch
- 1 tablespoon water
- 1 pinch nutmeg
- 1 pinch white pepper
- Optional: 1 tablespoon kirsch (cherry brandy)
- For dipping: Cubed crusty bread, raw veggies, steamed potatoes, etc.

Directions:

1. Rub the inside of the Instant Pot with the halved garlic clove. Discard the garlic afterward.
2. Combine the grated cheese with the wine and lemon juice in the Instant Pot.
3. In a small bowl, mix the cornstarch with water to create a slurry. Pour this into the Instant Pot, stirring well.
4. Secure the Instant Pot lid and set the device to manual, low pressure for 4 minutes. After cooking, use a quick release to release the pressure.
5. Open the lid and stir the mixture, seasoning with nutmeg, white pepper, and kirsch (if using). Use the 'Keep Warm' function to maintain the fondue's temperature while serving. Stir occasionally and serve with chosen dippers.

Nutritional Information: 380 calories, 25g protein, 5g carbohydrates, 28g fat, 0g fiber, 95mg cholesterol, 250mg sodium, 150mg potassium.

Herb & Garlic Cream Cheese Spread

Yield: 4 servings | Prep time: 10 minutes | Cook time: 15 minutes

Ingredients:

- 2 cups whole milk
- 3 tablespoons lemon juice
- 2 garlic cloves, minced
- 1 tablespoon fresh dill, chopped
- 1 tablespoon fresh chives, chopped
- 1 tablespoon fresh parsley, chopped
- Salt to taste
- Freshly ground black pepper to taste

Directions:

1. Pour the whole milk into the Instant Pot and press the 'Sauté' button. Heat the milk until it reaches about 190°F (just before boiling), then turn off the Instant Pot.
2. Stir in the lemon juice gently, allowing the milk to curdle. Let it sit for about 5 minutes.
3. Using a fine-mesh strainer, strain out the liquid, leaving the curdled milk solids behind. This is your fresh cream cheese base.
4. Transfer the cream cheese to a bowl, and mix in the minced garlic, dill, chives, and parsley. Season with salt and pepper.
5. Chill in the refrigerator for at least 1 hour before serving to allow the flavors to meld together.

Nutritional Information: 110 calories, 6g protein, 8g carbohydrates, 6g fat, 0g fiber, 25mg cholesterol, 85mg sodium, 230mg potassium.

Instant Pot Paneer

Yield: 4 servings | Prep time: 5 minutes | Cook time: 25 minutes

Ingredients:

- 8 cups whole milk
- 2-3 tablespoons lemon juice or white vinegar

Directions:

1. Pour the whole milk into the Instant Pot. Select the "Yogurt" setting and adjust to the "Boil" mode.
2. Once the Instant Pot signals that the boiling is done, carefully open the lid. Stir the milk and ensure it's fully heated to about 200°F.
3. Slowly add the lemon juice or vinegar while stirring gently, allowing the milk to curdle. Allow it to sit for about 10 minutes.
4. Line a strainer with a clean cheesecloth or muslin cloth and place it over a bowl. Pour the curdled milk mixture into the cloth to separate the whey from the paneer.
5. Gather the ends of the cloth and squeeze gently to remove any excess whey. Shape it into a block and place a heavy weight on top for about 1 hour to set.

Nutritional Information: 300 calories, 16g protein, 12g carbohydrates, 20g fat, 0g fiber, 50mg cholesterol, 125mg sodium, 520mg potassium.

Mediterranean Yogurt with Nuts & Honey

Yield: 4 servings | Prep time: 5 minutes | Cook time: 8 hours (mostly inactive for yogurt setting)

Ingredients:

- 4 cups whole milk
- 2 tablespoons yogurt starter or plain yogurt with active cultures
- 2 tablespoons honey
- ¼ cup mixed nuts (e.g., walnuts, almonds, pistachios), roughly chopped
- A pinch of sea salt

Directions:

1. Pour the milk into the Instant Pot. Select the "Yogurt" setting and adjust to the "Boil" mode.
2. Once boiling is done and milk has cooled to about 110°F, whisk in the yogurt starter or plain yogurt.
3. Cover the Instant Pot with its lid (ensure the vent is set to the sealing position). Set the pot to the "Yogurt" setting and adjust the time for 8 hours or until yogurt is thickened to your liking.
4. After the yogurt has set, gently mix in the honey and sea salt. Divide into serving bowls.
5. Garnish each serving with a generous sprinkle of mixed nuts before serving.

Nutritional Information: 230 calories, 10g protein, 23g carbohydrates, 11g fat, 1g fiber, 25mg cholesterol, 80mg sodium, 350mg potassium.

Brie & Roasted Garlic Dip

Yield: 4 servings | Prep time: 10 minutes | Cook time: 30 minutes

Ingredients:

- 1 whole garlic bulb, top trimmed to expose cloves
- 1 teaspoon olive oil
- 8 oz. Brie cheese, rind removed and cut into chunks
- 1 tablespoon fresh thyme leaves
- 1 tablespoon fresh rosemary, finely chopped
- Salt and freshly ground black pepper to taste
- Fresh parsley, for garnish (optional)

Directions:

1. Drizzle olive oil over the exposed garlic cloves. Place the garlic bulb on a piece of foil and wrap it up.
2. Pour one cup of water into the Instant Pot and place the trivet inside. Put the wrapped garlic bulb on the trivet. Close the lid and set to pressure cook on high for 15 minutes.
3. Once done, let the pressure release naturally. Carefully open the lid, remove the garlic bulb and let it cool slightly.
4. In a mixing bowl, squeeze out the roasted garlic cloves and mash them with a fork. Add Brie cheese, thyme, rosemary, salt, and pepper. Mix until well combined.
5. Transfer the mixture back into the Instant Pot, set it to "Sauté" mode, and stir constantly until the cheese is melted and combined with the garlic. Garnish with parsley if desired.

Nutritional Information: 180 calories, 10g protein, 5g carbohydrates, 14g fat, 0.5g fiber, 45mg cholesterol, 200mg sodium, 150mg potassium.

Flavorful Sides & Accents

Olive & Herb Focaccia

Yield: 6 servings | Prep time: 90 minutes (including dough rise time) | Cook time: 30 minutes

Ingredients:

- 3 cups all-purpose flour
- 1 packet (2 1/4 tsp) active dry yeast
- 1 1/2 cups warm water (110°F)
- 2 tbsp olive oil, plus extra for drizzling
- 1 tsp salt
- 1/2 cup pitted Kalamata olives, chopped
- 1 tbsp fresh rosemary, finely chopped
- 1 tbsp fresh thyme leaves
- 1 tsp coarse sea salt, for sprinkling

Directions:

1. In a bowl, dissolve the yeast in warm water. Allow it to sit for 5 minutes until frothy. Add in the flour, olive oil, and 1 tsp of salt. Mix until a dough forms.
2. Knead the dough on a floured surface until smooth. Place it back into the bowl, cover with a cloth, and let it rise for 1 hour, or until it has doubled in size.
3. Once risen, punch down the dough and press it into a greased springform pan or similar that fits into the Instant Pot.
4. Push olives into the dough and sprinkle with rosemary, thyme, and coarse sea salt. Drizzle with additional olive oil.
5. Pour 1 cup of water into the Instant Pot, place the trivet inside, and set the pan on top. Close the lid, set the Instant Pot to steam mode, and cook for 30 minutes. Once done, let it cool slightly before serving.

Nutritional Information: 320 calories, 8g protein, 58g carbohydrates, 7g fat, 2g fiber, 0mg cholesterol, 500mg sodium, 75mg potassium.

Garlic & Parmesan Mashed Potatoes

Yield: 4 servings | Prep time: 15 minutes | Cook time: 12 minutes

Ingredients:

- 2 pounds russet potatoes, peeled and cut into equal-sized pieces
- 4 cloves garlic, minced
- 1 cup water
- 1/2 cup grated Parmesan cheese
- 1/4 cup extra virgin olive oil
- 1/2 teaspoon salt (adjust to taste)
- 1/4 teaspoon black pepper (adjust to taste)
- 2 tablespoons fresh chives, chopped (optional for garnish)

Directions:

1. Place the potato pieces, garlic, and water into the Instant Pot. Secure the lid and set to manual mode. Cook on high pressure for 12 minutes.
2. After the cooking time is complete, release the pressure immediately and drain any remaining water from the pot.
3. Add the Parmesan cheese, olive oil, salt, and pepper to the pot. Mash the potatoes using a potato masher or an electric mixer until smooth and creamy. Adjust salt and pepper to taste.
4. Transfer to a serving dish and garnish with chives, if desired. Serve hot.

Nutritional Information: 330 calories, 8g protein, 45g carbohydrates, 14g fat, 3g fiber, 10mg cholesterol, 500mg sodium, 950mg potassium.

Instant Marinated Olives

Yield: 4 servings | Prep time: 10 minutes | Cook time: 5 minutes

Ingredients:

- 2 cups mixed olives (such as Kalamata, green, and black olives)
- 4 cloves garlic, thinly sliced
- 1/2 cup extra virgin olive oil
- 1/4 cup fresh lemon juice
- 1 tablespoon fresh rosemary, finely chopped
- 1 tablespoon fresh thyme leaves
- 1/2 teaspoon red chili flakes (optional for a little kick)
- Zest of 1 lemon
- 1 bay leaf

Directions:

1. In the Instant Pot, combine olives, garlic, olive oil, lemon juice, rosemary, thyme, chili flakes (if using), lemon zest, and bay leaf.
2. Close the lid, set the valve to the sealing position, and select the "Warm" setting. Let the olives marinate for 5 minutes in the warm oil mixture.
3. Release any pressure (though there shouldn't be much), open the lid, and give the olives a good stir to ensure they're well coated in the marinade.
4. Transfer the olives and marinade to a bowl or jar. They can be served immediately but are best when allowed to marinate in the refrigerator for at least a few hours or overnight.

Nutritional Information: 220 calories, 1g protein, 4g carbohydrates, 23g fat, 3g fiber, 0mg cholesterol, 800mg sodium, 50mg potassium.

Mediterranean Pickled Vegetables

Yield: 4 servings | Prep time: 15 minutes | Cook time: 5 minutes

Ingredients:

- 2 cups cauliflower florets
- 1 red bell pepper, sliced into thin strips
- 2 medium carrots, peeled and sliced into thin rounds
- 3 celery stalks, sliced
- 4 garlic cloves, peeled and lightly smashed
- 1 1/2 cups white vinegar or apple cider vinegar
- 1 1/2 cups water
- 2 tablespoons sea salt
- 1 tablespoon sugar
- 1 teaspoon coriander seeds
- 1 teaspoon black peppercorns
- 1 bay leaf
- 1/4 cup fresh dill, roughly chopped
- 1/4 cup fresh parsley, roughly chopped

Directions:

1. In the Instant Pot, combine vinegar, water, sea salt, sugar, coriander seeds, black peppercorns, and bay leaf. Stir until the salt and sugar dissolve.
2. Add the cauliflower, bell pepper, carrots, celery, and garlic to the pot.
3. Close the lid, set the valve to sealing, and choose the "Pressure Cook" or "Manual" setting. Set the time for 5 minutes.
4. Once the cooking cycle is complete, release the pressure manually. Remove the lid and let the vegetables cool for a few minutes.
5. Transfer the vegetables and brine into glass jars, ensuring the brine covers the vegetables. Mix in the dill and parsley. Seal the jars and refrigerate for at least 24 hours before consuming. They will keep in the refrigerator for up to 2 weeks.

Nutritional Information: 60 calories, 2g protein, 13g carbohydrates, 0.5g fat, 4g fiber, 0mg cholesterol, 1740mg sodium, 390mg potassium.

Pressure-Cooked Polenta with Sun-Dried Tomatoes
Yield: 4 servings | Prep time: 10 minutes | Cook time: 20 minutes

Ingredients:

- 1 cup coarse-ground polenta (cornmeal)
- 4 cups water or vegetable broth
- 1/2 cup sun-dried tomatoes (not in oil), finely chopped
- 1/4 cup grated Parmesan cheese (optional for a dairy-free version)
- 2 tablespoons extra-virgin olive oil
- 1 garlic clove, minced
- Salt and black pepper to taste
- 2 tablespoons fresh basil, chopped (for garnish)

Directions:

1. In your Instant Pot, combine the polenta, water or broth, sun-dried tomatoes, and minced garlic. Stir well to ensure that the polenta is fully submerged in the liquid.
2. Secure the lid on the Instant Pot, set the valve to sealing, and choose the "Porridge" or "Manual" setting for 15 minutes.
3. Once the cooking cycle is complete, allow the pressure to release naturally for 5 minutes, then release any remaining pressure manually.
4. Stir the polenta, incorporating the olive oil and Parmesan cheese (if using). Adjust salt and black pepper to taste.
5. Serve the polenta in bowls, garnished with fresh basil.

Nutritional Information: 230 calories, 5g protein, 35g carbohydrates, 7g fat, 3g fiber, 5mg cholesterol, 200mg sodium, 390mg potassium.

Lemon & Herb Roasted Carrots
Yield: 4 servings | Prep time: 10 minutes | Cook time: 15 minutes

Ingredients:

- 1 pound of carrots, peeled and cut into 2-inch pieces
- 2 tablespoons extra-virgin olive oil
- Zest and juice of 1 lemon
- 2 garlic cloves, minced
- 1 tablespoon fresh rosemary, finely chopped
- 1 tablespoon fresh thyme, finely chopped
- Salt and pepper to taste
- 2 tablespoons fresh parsley, chopped (for garnish)

Directions:

1. In a mixing bowl, toss the carrot pieces with olive oil, lemon zest, lemon juice, minced garlic, rosemary, thyme, salt, and pepper until well-coated.
2. Pour 1 cup of water into the Instant Pot and place the trivet at the bottom. Arrange the seasoned carrot pieces on top of the trivet.
3. Secure the lid, set the valve to sealing, and select "Pressure Cook" or "Manual" on high for 5 minutes.
4. Once the cooking cycle is complete, quick release the pressure. Carefully open the lid, remove the carrots, and transfer to a serving dish.
5. Garnish with chopped parsley before serving.

Nutritional Information: 110 calories, 2g protein, 17g carbohydrates, 5g fat, 4g fiber, 0mg cholesterol, 80mg sodium, 490mg potassium.

Quick Mediterranean Slaw

Yield: 4 servings | Prep time: 15 minutes | Cook time: 0 minutes

Ingredients:

- 4 cups shredded cabbage (mix of green and red)
- 1 cup shredded carrot
- 1/2 cup chopped kalamata olives
- 1/4 cup chopped sun-dried tomatoes
- 1/4 cup crumbled feta cheese
- 2 tablespoons extra-virgin olive oil
- 1 tablespoon red wine vinegar
- 1 garlic clove, minced
- 1 teaspoon dried oregano
- Salt and pepper to taste
- 2 tablespoons chopped fresh parsley

Directions:

1. In a large mixing bowl, combine the shredded cabbage, shredded carrot, kalamata olives, sun-dried tomatoes, and feta cheese.
2. In a small bowl, whisk together the olive oil, red wine vinegar, minced garlic, oregano, salt, and pepper to create the dressing.
3. Pour the dressing over the vegetable mixture and toss until everything is well coated.
4. Garnish with fresh parsley before serving. Can be served immediately or refrigerated for 1 hour to let flavors meld.

Nutritional Information: 160 calories, 3g protein, 15g carbohydrates, 11g fat, 4g fiber, 8mg cholesterol, 320mg sodium, 400mg potassium.

Tomato & Basil Bruschetta

Yield: 4 servings | Prep time: 10 minutes | Cook time: 5 minutes

Ingredients:

- 4 ripe tomatoes, diced
- 1/4 cup fresh basil leaves, chopped
- 2 garlic cloves, minced
- 2 tablespoons extra-virgin olive oil
- 1 tablespoon balsamic vinegar
- Salt and pepper to taste
- 8 slices of whole-grain baguette or rustic bread
- 1 tablespoon olive oil (for brushing)

Directions:

1. In a mixing bowl, combine the diced tomatoes, chopped basil, minced garlic, extra-virgin olive oil, balsamic vinegar, salt, and pepper. Mix well and set aside to let flavors meld.
2. Brush each bread slice with a bit of olive oil on both sides. Place them on the trivet inside the Instant Pot.
3. Using the 'Sauté' mode on the Instant Pot, lightly toast each side of the bread slices until they're golden brown, approximately 2-3 minutes each side.
4. Once toasted, spoon the tomato mixture generously onto each bread slice. Serve immediately.

Nutritional Information: 200 calories, 5g protein, 28g carbohydrates, 8g fat, 3g fiber, 0mg cholesterol, 240mg sodium, 320mg potassium.

Herbed Butter Beans

Yield: 4 servings | Prep time: 10 minutes | Cook time: 30 minutes

Ingredients:

- 2 cups dried butter beans, soaked overnight
- 4 cups water or vegetable broth
- 2 tablespoons olive oil
- 1 onion, finely chopped
- 3 garlic cloves, minced
- 1 teaspoon rosemary, finely chopped
- 1 teaspoon thyme, finely chopped
- Salt and pepper to taste
- Zest and juice of 1 lemon
- 2 tablespoons fresh parsley, chopped

Directions:

1. Turn on the Instant Pot on 'Sauté' mode. Add the olive oil, onion, and garlic, sautéing until translucent.
2. Add the soaked butter beans, rosemary, thyme, lemon zest, and water or vegetable broth. Stir well to combine.
3. Close the lid, set the Instant Pot to 'Pressure Cook' or 'Manual' on high pressure for 25 minutes.
4. Once cooking is complete, release the pressure naturally. Stir in the lemon juice, fresh parsley, and season with salt and pepper. Serve warm.

Nutritional Information: 240 calories, 14g protein, 40g carbohydrates, 5g fat, 10g fiber, 0mg cholesterol, 50mg sodium, 700mg potassium.

Instant Pot Stuffed Grape Leaves

Yield: 4 servings | Prep time: 30 minutes | Cook time: 20 minutes

Ingredients:

- 30 grape leaves, rinsed and stems removed
- 1 cup short-grain rice, rinsed
- 1 large onion, finely chopped
- 1/4 cup fresh parsley, chopped
- 1/4 cup fresh dill, chopped
- 2 tablespoons fresh mint, chopped
- 2 tablespoons olive oil
- Juice of 1 lemon
- 1 teaspoon salt
- 1/2 teaspoon black pepper
- 2 cups vegetable broth or water
- 1 tablespoon olive oil (for drizzling)

Directions:

1. In a mixing bowl, combine the rice, onion, parsley, dill, mint, olive oil, lemon juice, salt, and pepper. Mix until all ingredients are well incorporated.
2. Place a grape leaf flat on a cutting board, shiny side down. Put a spoonful of the rice mixture in the center of the leaf. Fold the sides over the filling, then roll the leaf tightly.
3. Repeat with the remaining leaves and filling.
4. Place the stuffed grape leaves in a single layer inside the Instant Pot. Pour the vegetable broth or water over the grape leaves, ensuring they are submerged.
5. Close the lid, set the Instant Pot to 'Pressure Cook' or 'Manual' on high pressure for 20 minutes. Once cooking is complete, release the pressure naturally. Drizzle with olive oil and serve.

Nutritional Information: 220 calories, 5g protein, 40g carbohydrates, 7g fat, 3g fiber, 0mg cholesterol, 320mg sodium, 300mg potassium.

Holiday & Festive Feasts

Instant Pot Lamb for Easter

Yield: 6 servings | Prep time: 15 minutes | Cook time: 60 minutes

Ingredients:

- 2.5 lbs boneless leg of lamb
- 1 tablespoon olive oil
- 4 cloves garlic, minced
- 1 teaspoon rosemary, chopped
- 1 teaspoon thyme, chopped
- 1 teaspoon oregano, chopped
- 1 cup beef or vegetable broth
- Juice of 1 lemon
- Salt and pepper to taste
- 1 tablespoon fresh parsley, chopped (for garnish)

Directions:

1. In a small bowl, mix together the minced garlic, rosemary, thyme, oregano, salt, and pepper.
2. Rub the lamb with the olive oil and then the herb mixture, ensuring it's well-coated.
3. Set the Instant Pot to 'Sauté' mode and sear the lamb on all sides until it's browned.
4. Add the broth and lemon juice to the Instant Pot. Close the lid and set to 'Pressure Cook' or 'Manual' on high pressure for 60 minutes.
5. Once cooking is complete, allow for a natural pressure release. Remove the lamb, let it rest for a few minutes, then slice and garnish with fresh parsley before serving.

Nutritional Information: 420 calories, 38g protein, 3g carbohydrates, 28g fat, 0.5g fiber, 120mg cholesterol, 280mg sodium, 420mg potassium.

Quick Mediterranean Stuffed Turkey

Yield: 4 servings | Prep time: 20 minutes | Cook time: 25 minutes

Ingredients:

- 4 turkey breast cutlets (about 1.5 lbs)
- 1 cup fresh spinach, chopped
- 1/2 cup feta cheese, crumbled
- 1/4 cup sun-dried tomatoes, chopped
- 2 cloves garlic, minced
- 1 tablespoon olive oil
- 1/2 teaspoon dried oregano
- 1/2 teaspoon dried basil
- Salt and pepper to taste
- 1 cup chicken broth

Directions:

1. In a mixing bowl, combine the spinach, feta cheese, sun-dried tomatoes, garlic, oregano, and basil. Mix well.
2. Lay each turkey cutlet flat, season with salt and pepper, and place a portion of the spinach mixture in the center. Roll up and secure with toothpicks.
3. Set the Instant Pot to 'Sauté' mode and add olive oil. Once hot, sear each stuffed turkey cutlet on all sides until lightly browned.
4. Pour in the chicken broth. Close the lid and set to 'Pressure Cook' or 'Manual' on high pressure for 15 minutes.
5. Once cooking is complete, allow for a quick pressure release. Remove the turkey carefully, discarding toothpicks before serving.

Nutritional Information: 290 calories, 38g protein, 8g carbohydrates, 12g fat, 2g fiber, 90mg cholesterol, 400mg sodium, 420mg potassium.

Pressure-Cooked Christmas Seafood Medley

Yield: 4 servings | Prep time: 15 minutes | Cook time: 5 minutes

Ingredients:

- 1/2 lb fresh shrimp, peeled and deveined
- 1/2 lb mussels, cleaned
- 1/2 lb clams, cleaned
- 1/2 lb calamari rings
- 3 cloves garlic, minced
- 1 onion, finely chopped
- 1 cup cherry tomatoes, halved
- 1/4 cup fresh parsley, chopped
- 2 tablespoons olive oil
- 1 cup white wine
- 1 lemon, juiced
- Salt and pepper to taste
- 1 pinch saffron threads (optional)
- 1 teaspoon red pepper flakes

Directions:

1. Set the Instant Pot to 'Sauté' mode. Add olive oil, garlic, and onion. Cook until onions are translucent.
2. Add white wine, cherry tomatoes, lemon juice, saffron (if using), and red pepper flakes. Stir well and let simmer for a minute.
3. Add in the seafood - shrimp, mussels, clams, and calamari. Mix to ensure the seafood is well-coated with the sauce.
4. Close the lid, set the Instant Pot to 'Manual' or 'Pressure Cook' mode on high pressure for 5 minutes. Once done, allow for a quick pressure release.
5. Open the lid, discard any unopened mussels or clams, garnish with fresh parsley, and serve immediately.

Nutritional Information: 260 calories, 24g protein, 10g carbohydrates, 8g fat, 1g fiber, 170mg cholesterol, 500mg sodium, 550mg potassium.

Festive Olive & Fig Roast Pork

Yield: 4 servings | Prep time: 20 minutes | Cook time: 40 minutes

Ingredients:

- 2 lbs pork tenderloin
- 1 cup dried figs, chopped
- 1/2 cup Kalamata olives, pitted and chopped
- 4 cloves garlic, minced
- 2 tablespoons fresh rosemary, chopped
- 2 tablespoons olive oil
- 1/2 cup white wine
- 1/2 cup chicken broth
- Salt and pepper to taste
- Zest of 1 lemon

Directions:

1. In a bowl, combine chopped figs, olives, garlic, rosemary, and lemon zest. Season with salt and pepper and mix well to create the stuffing.
2. Make a deep slit along the side of the pork tenderloin, being careful not to cut through. Stuff the pork with the fig and olive mixture.
3. Set the Instant Pot to 'Sauté' mode and add olive oil. Brown the pork on all sides, about 3-4 minutes per side.
4. Pour in white wine and chicken broth. Set the Instant Pot to 'Manual' or 'Pressure Cook' mode on high pressure for 40 minutes. Allow a natural pressure release before opening.
5. Once cooked, let the pork rest for a few minutes before slicing. Serve with sauce from the pot drizzled on top.

Nutritional Information: 420 calories, 35g protein, 28g carbohydrates, 15g fat, 4g fiber, 110mg cholesterol, 450mg sodium, 640mg potassium.

Holiday Beef & Olive Tagine

Yield: 4 servings | Prep time: 25 minutes | Cook time: 45 minutes

Ingredients:

- 1.5 lbs beef stew meat, cut into 1-inch chunks
- 1 cup green olives, pitted and halved
- 1 large onion, finely chopped
- 3 cloves garlic, minced
- 2 tablespoons olive oil
- 2 teaspoons ground cumin
- 1 teaspoon ground ginger
- 1 teaspoon paprika
- 1/2 teaspoon ground cinnamon
- 1/4 teaspoon saffron threads (optional)
- 1 cup beef broth
- 1 can (14 oz) diced tomatoes
- 1/4 cup fresh cilantro, chopped
- Zest of 1 lemon
- Salt and pepper to taste

Directions:

1. In the Instant Pot, select the 'Sauté' function. Add olive oil, onions, and garlic, and sauté until softened.
2. Add beef chunks, browning them on all sides. Add the cumin, ginger, paprika, cinnamon, and saffron, mixing well to coat the beef.
3. Pour in beef broth and diced tomatoes, followed by the olives. Mix well.
4. Close the lid and set the Instant Pot to 'Manual' or 'Pressure Cook' mode on high pressure for 45 minutes. Allow a natural release before opening the lid.
5. Stir in the fresh cilantro and lemon zest just before serving. Adjust seasoning with salt and pepper if necessary.

Nutritional Information: 460 calories, 40g protein, 20g carbohydrates, 24g fat, 4g fiber, 105mg cholesterol, 600mg sodium, 720mg potassium.

Instant New Year's Lentil Stew

Yield: 4 servings | Prep time: 15 minutes | Cook time: 30 minutes

Ingredients:

- 1 cup dried green lentils, rinsed and drained
- 1 large onion, diced
- 3 cloves garlic, minced
- 2 carrots, peeled and diced
- 2 celery stalks, diced
- 1 bell pepper, diced (color of choice)
- 1 can (14 oz) diced tomatoes
- 4 cups vegetable broth
- 2 tablespoons olive oil
- 1 teaspoon ground cumin
- 1 teaspoon smoked paprika
- 1/2 teaspoon dried thyme
- Salt and pepper to taste
- 2 tablespoons fresh parsley, chopped (for garnish)
- Zest of 1 lemon

Directions:

1. Using the 'Sauté' function on the Instant Pot, add olive oil, onions, garlic, carrots, celery, and bell pepper. Sauté until the onions are translucent.
2. Stir in cumin, smoked paprika, thyme, salt, and pepper. Mix well.
3. Add lentils, diced tomatoes, and vegetable broth to the pot, ensuring the lentils are submerged in the liquid.
4. Close the Instant Pot lid, setting the valve to sealing. Set the Instant Pot to 'Manual' or 'Pressure Cook' on high pressure for 30 minutes. After cooking, allow a natural release for 10 minutes before manually releasing the remaining pressure.
5. Stir in the lemon zest and adjust seasoning if necessary. Serve in bowls garnished with fresh parsley.

Nutritional Information: 280 calories, 15g protein, 40g carbohydrates, 7g fat, 16g fiber, 0mg cholesterol, 580mg sodium, 800mg potassium.

Chicken with Dates & Pistachios
Yield: 4 servings | Prep time: 20 minutes | Cook time: 25 minutes

Ingredients:

- 4 boneless, skinless chicken breasts
- 1 cup dates, pitted and chopped
- 1/2 cup pistachios, shelled and roughly chopped
- 2 cloves garlic, minced
- 1 onion, finely sliced
- 1 teaspoon ground cinnamon
- 1/2 teaspoon ground turmeric
- 1/2 teaspoon ground cumin
- 2 tablespoons olive oil
- 1 cup chicken broth
- Salt and pepper to taste
- Fresh parsley, for garnish
- Zest of 1 lemon

Directions:

1. Using the 'Sauté' function on the Instant Pot, heat the olive oil and add the onion and garlic. Sauté until translucent.
2. Season chicken breasts with salt, pepper, cinnamon, turmeric, and cumin. Add them to the Instant Pot and brown each side for about 3 minutes.
3. Pour in the chicken broth, then add the dates and pistachios. Stir gently to mix the ingredients.
4. Seal the Instant Pot lid, set the valve to sealing, and cook on 'Manual' or 'Pressure Cook' for 20 minutes on high pressure. Allow a natural release for 5 minutes before manually releasing the remaining pressure.
5. Serve the chicken with sauce, garnished with fresh parsley and lemon zest.

Nutritional Information: 480 calories, 40g protein, 35g carbohydrates, 20g fat, 5g fiber, 95mg cholesterol, 420mg sodium, 700mg potassium.

Mediterranean Festive Vegetable Platter
Yield: 4 servings | Prep time: 15 minutes | Cook time: 8 minutes

Ingredients:

- 1 red bell pepper, sliced into strips
- 1 zucchini, sliced into rounds
- 1 yellow squash, sliced into rounds
- 10 asparagus spears, trimmed
- 1 red onion, cut into wedges
- 10 cherry tomatoes
- 4 garlic cloves, minced
- 2 tablespoons olive oil
- 1 teaspoon dried oregano
- 1 teaspoon dried basil
- Salt and pepper to taste
- 1/4 cup fresh parsley, chopped
- 1 tablespoon balsamic vinegar
- 1/4 cup crumbled feta cheese (optional)

Directions:

1. In a mixing bowl, toss together red bell pepper, zucchini, yellow squash, asparagus, red onion, and cherry tomatoes with olive oil, garlic, oregano, basil, salt, and pepper.
2. Turn on the 'Sauté' function of the Instant Pot and add the vegetable mixture. Sauté for 3-4 minutes, just to give them a little color.
3. Lock the Instant Pot lid and set the valve to sealing. Choose the 'Steam' function and set for 4 minutes.
4. Once the cooking cycle is complete, perform a quick release. Transfer the vegetables to a serving platter.
5. Drizzle with balsamic vinegar, sprinkle with fresh parsley and, if desired, crumbled feta cheese.

Nutritional Information: 140 calories, 4g protein, 18g carbohydrates, 7g fat, 4g fiber, 8mg cholesterol, 110mg sodium, 520mg potassium.

Lamb & Apricot for Eid Celebrations

Yield: 4 servings | Prep time: 20 minutes | Cook time: 40 minutes

Ingredients:

- 1 lb lamb, cut into bite-sized chunks
- 1 cup dried apricots, halved
- 1 large onion, finely chopped
- 2 garlic cloves, minced
- 2 tablespoons olive oil
- 1 teaspoon ground cumin
- 1 teaspoon ground coriander
- 1/2 teaspoon ground cinnamon
- 1/4 teaspoon ground cardamom
- 2 cups beef or chicken broth
- Salt and pepper to taste
- 1/4 cup fresh cilantro, chopped
- 1/4 cup slivered almonds, toasted
- Zest of 1 lemon

Directions:

1. Turn on the 'Sauté' function of the Instant Pot and add olive oil. Once hot, brown the lamb chunks on all sides, then remove and set aside.
2. In the same pot, add onions and garlic, sautéing until translucent. Stir in the cumin, coriander, cinnamon, and cardamom, cooking for another minute until fragrant.
3. Return the browned lamb to the pot, adding apricots and broth. Season with salt and pepper.
4. Lock the Instant Pot lid, set the valve to sealing, and select the 'Meat/Stew' setting for 35 minutes. Once completed, allow a natural release for 10 minutes, then quick release.
5. Serve garnished with fresh cilantro, toasted almonds, and lemon zest.

Nutritional Information: 410 calories, 28g protein, 33g carbohydrates, 18g fat, 4g fiber, 80mg cholesterol, 550mg sodium, 800mg potassium.

Quick Festive Mediterranean Rice

Yield: 4 servings | Prep time: 10 minutes | Cook time: 12 minutes

Ingredients:

- 1 cup Basmati rice, rinsed and drained
- 1 1/4 cups chicken or vegetable broth
- 2 tablespoons olive oil
- 1 medium onion, finely chopped
- 2 garlic cloves, minced
- 1/2 cup cherry tomatoes, halved
- 1/4 cup pitted Kalamata olives, chopped
- 1/4 cup dried currants or raisins
- 1/4 cup pine nuts, toasted
- Zest and juice of 1 lemon
- 2 tablespoons fresh parsley, chopped
- Salt and pepper to taste

Directions:

1. Using the 'Sauté' function of the Instant Pot, heat olive oil and sauté onions until translucent. Add garlic and sauté for another minute.
2. Add the rice to the pot, stirring for a minute to coat the grains with oil. Pour in the broth, ensuring the rice is fully submerged. Season with salt and pepper.
3. Lock the Instant Pot lid, set the valve to sealing, and select the 'Rice' setting, which typically cooks for 12 minutes.
4. Once completed, allow a natural release for 5 minutes, then quick release. Fluff the rice and fold in cherry tomatoes, olives, currants/raisins, pine nuts, lemon zest, and juice. Garnish with fresh parsley before serving.

Nutritional Information: 320 calories, 6g protein, 50g carbohydrates, 12g fat, 3g fiber, 0mg cholesterol, 280mg sodium, 350mg potassium.

Quick Mediterranean Bites

Instant Pot Greek Meatballs

Yield: 4 servings | Prep time: 20 minutes | Cook time: 8 minutes

Ingredients:

- 1 lb ground lamb (or beef)
- 1/2 cup breadcrumbs
- 1/4 cup fresh parsley, finely chopped
- 1/4 cup fresh mint, finely chopped
- 1 medium onion, grated
- 3 garlic cloves, minced
- 1 large egg
- Zest of 1 lemon
- 1 teaspoon dried oregano
- Salt and pepper to taste
- 1 tablespoon olive oil
- 1/2 cup chicken or beef broth

Directions:

1. In a large mixing bowl, combine ground lamb, breadcrumbs, parsley, mint, onion, garlic, egg, lemon zest, oregano, salt, and pepper. Mix until just combined.
2. Shape the mixture into meatballs, each about 1-inch in diameter.
3. Turn the Instant Pot on 'Sauté' mode and heat the olive oil. Brown the meatballs in batches, ensuring all sides are seared.
4. Once all meatballs are browned, pour in the broth, close the Instant Pot lid, set the valve to sealing, and cook on 'Manual' or 'Pressure Cook' for 8 minutes.
5. Allow a natural release for 5 minutes, then perform a quick release. Serve with a tzatziki sauce or on a bed of rice or salad.

Nutritional Information: 380 calories, 22g protein, 20g carbohydrates, 24g fat, 2g fiber, 90mg cholesterol, 400mg sodium, 300mg potassium.

Pressure-Cooked Stuffed Mushrooms

Yield: 4 servings | Prep time: 15 minutes | Cook time: 8 minutes

Ingredients:

- 16 large white mushrooms, stems removed and finely chopped, caps reserved
- 1/2 cup feta cheese, crumbled
- 1/4 cup breadcrumbs
- 2 tablespoons fresh parsley, finely chopped
- 2 garlic cloves, minced
- 1/4 cup sun-dried tomatoes, finely chopped
- 1/4 cup red onion, finely chopped
- 2 tablespoons olive oil
- Salt and pepper to taste
- 1/2 cup vegetable broth

Directions:

1. In a mixing bowl, combine chopped mushroom stems, feta cheese, breadcrumbs, parsley, garlic, sun-dried tomatoes, and red onion. Mix until well combined. Season with salt and pepper to taste.
2. Carefully stuff each mushroom cap with the mixture, pressing gently to pack the filling.
3. Pour vegetable broth into the Instant Pot. Place the trivet or a steamer basket at the bottom and arrange the stuffed mushrooms on top.
4. Secure the lid, set the valve to sealing, and cook on 'Manual' or 'Pressure Cook' for 8 minutes.
5. Allow a natural release for 5 minutes, then perform a quick release. Carefully remove the mushrooms and serve warm.

Nutritional Information: 150 calories, 6g protein, 14g carbohydrates, 8g fat, 2g fiber, 15mg cholesterol, 320mg sodium, 420mg potassium.

Quick Olive & Cheese Pinwheels

Yield: 4 servings | Prep time: 10 minutes | Cook time: 15 minutes

Ingredients:

- 1 sheet puff pastry, thawed
- 1/2 cup green olives, pitted and finely chopped
- 1/2 cup feta cheese, crumbled
- 2 tablespoons fresh basil, finely chopped
- 2 tablespoons olive oil
- 1/2 teaspoon black pepper
- 1 egg (for egg wash)
- 1 tablespoon water (for egg wash)

Directions:

1. Lay out the puff pastry sheet flat on a lightly floured surface. Brush it lightly with olive oil.
2. Spread the chopped olives, crumbled feta, and fresh basil evenly over the pastry. Season with black pepper.
3. Carefully roll the pastry into a tight log. Slice the log into 1-inch pinwheels.
4. In a bowl, whisk together the egg and water to make an egg wash. Brush each pinwheel lightly with the egg wash.
5. Place the pinwheels on the trivet or a steamer basket inside the Instant Pot. Add 1 cup of water to the pot, secure the lid, and set to 'Steam' for 15 minutes. Once done, perform a quick release.

Nutritional Information: 280 calories, 7g protein, 25g carbohydrates, 18g fat, 1g fiber, 35mg cholesterol, 480mg sodium, 120mg potassium.

Instant Pot Falafel

Yield: 4 servings | Prep time: 15 minutes (excluding overnight soaking) | Cook time: 10 minutes

Ingredients:

- 2 cups dried chickpeas, soaked overnight and drained
- 1 medium onion, roughly chopped
- 4 garlic cloves
- 1/4 cup fresh parsley, finely chopped
- 1/4 cup fresh cilantro, finely chopped
- 2 teaspoons ground cumin
- 1 teaspoon ground coriander
- 1/2 teaspoon cayenne pepper
- 1 teaspoon salt
- 1/2 teaspoon baking powder
- 2 tablespoons all-purpose flour
- 1/4 cup water
- Olive oil (for drizzling)

Directions:

1. In a food processor, combine soaked chickpeas, onion, garlic, parsley, cilantro, cumin, coriander, cayenne, and salt. Process until smooth.
2. Add baking powder and flour, then pulse until the mixture forms a dough. Shape into small balls.
3. Pour 1/4 cup of water into the Instant Pot and place a trivet or steamer basket at the bottom. Arrange falafel balls on the trivet, ensuring they don't touch.
4. Secure the Instant Pot lid and set the vent to 'Sealing'. Cook on 'Steam' mode for 10 minutes. Once done, perform a quick release.
5. Before serving, optionally drizzle or brush with olive oil for added flavor.

Nutritional Information: 315 calories, 15g protein, 55g carbohydrates, 5g fat, 14g fiber, 0mg cholesterol, 630mg sodium, 770mg potassium.

Mediterranean Tapas Platter

Yield: 4 servings | Prep time: 20 minutes | Cook time: 10 minutes

Ingredients:

- 1 cup green olives, pitted
- 1 cup kalamata olives, pitted
- 4 garlic cloves, minced
- Zest of 1 lemon
- 1 tablespoon fresh rosemary, minced
- 1 cup cherry tomatoes
- 1 cup artichoke hearts, drained
- 1/2 cup feta cheese, cubed
- 1 cup hummus (store-bought or homemade)
- 1 tablespoon olive oil
- 1 teaspoon smoked paprika
- Salt, to taste
- Fresh parsley, chopped (for garnish)

Directions:

1. In the Instant Pot, combine green olives, kalamata olives, garlic, lemon zest, rosemary, and olive oil. Gently stir to combine.
2. Secure the Instant Pot lid and set the vent to 'Sealing'. Cook on 'Manual' mode or 'Pressure Cook' on high for 3 minutes. Once done, perform a quick release.
3. Allow the olive mixture to cool slightly. Arrange the olives, cherry tomatoes, artichoke hearts, feta cheese, and hummus on a serving platter.
4. Sprinkle smoked paprika over the hummus and garnish with fresh parsley. Season with salt as needed.

Nutritional Information: 250 calories, 8g protein, 20g carbohydrates, 18g fat, 7g fiber, 15mg cholesterol, 800mg sodium, 400mg potassium.

Quick Spinach & Cheese Triangles

Yield: 4 servings | Prep time: 15 minutes | Cook time: 10 minutes

Ingredients:

- 2 cups fresh spinach, chopped
- 1 cup feta cheese, crumbled
- 1/4 cup parmesan cheese, grated
- 1/4 cup fresh dill, chopped
- 1 garlic clove, minced
- 1 tablespoon olive oil
- 1/4 teaspoon black pepper
- 1/4 teaspoon nutmeg
- 8 sheets of phyllo dough, cut into triangles
- Additional olive oil for brushing

Directions:

1. Turn on the Instant Pot to 'Sauté' mode and add 1 tablespoon of olive oil. Once hot, add the garlic and sauté until fragrant. Add the spinach and sauté until wilted.
2. Transfer the spinach to a bowl and let it cool slightly. Once cooled, mix in feta cheese, parmesan, dill, pepper, and nutmeg until well combined.
3. Place a spoonful of the spinach and cheese mixture on the wide end of a phyllo triangle. Fold the phyllo over the filling to form a smaller triangle, then keep folding until the end of the sheet, making sure to keep the triangle shape.
4. Place the triangles on the Instant Pot's steaming rack, ensuring they don't touch. Close the lid, set the vent to 'Sealing', and pressure cook on high for 10 minutes. Once done, perform a quick release.

Nutritional Information: 280 calories, 10g protein, 25g carbohydrates, 15g fat, 2g fiber, 40mg cholesterol, 600mg sodium, 300mg potassium.

Pressure-Cooked Garlic Shrimp

Yield: 4 servings | Prep time: 10 minutes | Cook time: 3 minutes

Ingredients:

- 1 lb large shrimp, peeled and deveined
- 6 garlic cloves, minced
- 1/4 cup extra virgin olive oil
- 1/4 teaspoon red pepper flakes
- 1/4 cup fresh parsley, chopped
- Zest and juice of 1 lemon
- Salt and pepper to taste

Directions:

1. In the Instant Pot, combine olive oil, minced garlic, and red pepper flakes. Use the 'Sauté' mode to heat the mixture until fragrant.
2. Add the shrimp, ensuring they are evenly spread in the pot. Season with salt, pepper, and half of the lemon zest.
3. Lock the lid, set the vent to 'Sealing', and pressure cook on high for 3 minutes. Once done, perform a quick release.
4. Stir in lemon juice, remaining lemon zest, and fresh parsley. Serve immediately.

Nutritional Information: 240 calories, 24g protein, 3g carbohydrates, 15g fat, 0.2g fiber, 180mg cholesterol, 580mg sodium, 250mg potassium.

Mediterranean Quesadillas

Yield: 4 servings | Prep time: 15 minutes | Cook time: 5 minutes

Ingredients:

- 4 large whole wheat tortillas
- 1 cup feta cheese, crumbled
- 1/2 cup Kalamata olives, pitted and chopped
- 1 cup fresh spinach, chopped
- 1/2 cup roasted red bell peppers, sliced
- 1/2 cup artichoke hearts, chopped
- 1/4 cup red onion, finely diced
- 2 tbsp extra virgin olive oil
- Salt and pepper to taste

Directions:

1. Lay out the tortillas and evenly distribute feta cheese, olives, spinach, roasted bell peppers, artichoke hearts, and red onion onto one half of each tortilla.
2. Season the fillings with salt and pepper, then fold over the tortilla to create a half-moon shape.
3. Turn the Instant Pot to 'Sauté' mode and add olive oil. Once hot, place one quesadilla at a time, cooking for 2-3 minutes on each side or until golden brown and the cheese has melted.
4. Remove and slice into wedges. Repeat with the remaining quesadillas.

Nutritional Information: 365 calories, 11g protein, 42g carbohydrates, 18g fat, 7g fiber, 25mg cholesterol, 690mg sodium, 320mg potassium.

Olive & Tomato Mini Pizzas
Yield: 4 servings | Prep time: 15 minutes | Cook time: 10 minutes

Ingredients:

- 4 small whole wheat pita bread rounds
- 1 cup cherry tomatoes, halved
- 1/2 cup Kalamata olives, pitted and sliced
- 1/2 cup mozzarella cheese, shredded
- 1/4 cup feta cheese, crumbled
- 2 tbsp extra virgin olive oil
- 1 tsp dried oregano
- 1 tsp dried basil
- Salt and pepper to taste
- Fresh basil leaves for garnish (optional)

Directions:

1. Spread each pita bread round with a thin layer of olive oil. Sprinkle with oregano, basil, salt, and pepper.
2. Distribute cherry tomato halves and sliced olives evenly among the pita rounds.
3. Sprinkle mozzarella and feta cheese over the tomatoes and olives on each pita.
4. Place the mini pizzas on the Instant Pot trivet with a cup of water below. Close the lid and set to 'Manual' mode, high pressure for 10 minutes. Once done, do a quick release.
5. Carefully remove the mini pizzas from the Instant Pot, garnish with fresh basil leaves if desired, and serve hot.

Nutritional Information: 310 calories, 12g protein, 34g carbohydrates, 15g fat, 5g fiber, 25mg cholesterol, 520mg sodium, 220mg potassium.

Instant Pot Mini Lamb Pies
Yield: 4 servings | Prep time: 20 minutes | Cook time: 25 minutes

Ingredients:

- 1 lb ground lamb
- 1 medium onion, finely chopped
- 2 cloves garlic, minced
- 1/2 cup Kalamata olives, chopped
- 1/4 cup feta cheese, crumbled
- 1 tsp dried oregano
- 1 tsp dried rosemary
- 1/2 tsp ground cumin
- 1/4 tsp ground cinnamon
- 2 tbsp tomato paste
- 1 cup beef or vegetable broth
- Salt and pepper to taste
- 1 package of puff pastry or pie dough, thawed
- 1 egg, beaten (for egg wash)

Directions:

1. On 'Sauté' mode in the Instant Pot, cook the ground lamb until browned. Add onion and garlic, sautéing until softened. Mix in olives, spices, and tomato paste.
2. Pour in the broth and let the mixture simmer until thickened. Stir in feta cheese and then turn off the Instant Pot. Let the filling cool slightly.
3. Roll out the puff pastry or pie dough and cut circles to fit into a muffin tin. Place each circle into a muffin slot, then fill with the lamb mixture.
4. Cover each pie with another circle of dough, pressing the edges to seal. Brush the top with the beaten egg.
5. Place the muffin tin on the Instant Pot trivet with a cup of water below. Close the lid and set to 'Manual' mode, high pressure for 20 minutes. Once done, do a quick release.

Nutritional Information: 530 calories, 22g protein, 40g carbohydrates, 31g fat, 2g fiber, 85mg cholesterol, 580mg sodium, 370mg potassium.

Copyright © 2023 by Emmett Carlson.

All rights reserved. No part of this cookbook may be reproduced, distributed, or transmitted in any form or by any means, including photocopying, recording, or other electronic or mechanical methods, without the prior written permission of the author, except in the case of brief quotations embodied in critical reviews and certain other noncommercial uses permitted by copyright law.

The recipes and advice presented in this cookbook are intended for informational purposes only. The author is not a licensed dietitian, and the information contained in this cookbook should not be considered a substitute for professional medical advice, diagnosis, or treatment. The author disclaims any liability or responsibility for any loss or damage caused or alleged to be caused, directly or indirectly, by the use or misuse of any information contained in this cookbook.

By using this cookbook, you acknowledge that you have read and understand the information presented in this copyright and disclaimer statement, and you agree to be bound by the terms and conditions set forth herein.

Made in the USA
Las Vegas, NV
13 October 2023